Downtown Burlington, 1860, as viewed from
the steeple of the First Unitarian Church.

Vermont Album

A drive in the country west of Woodstock. Circa 1900.

Vermont Album

A COLLECTION OF EARLY VERMONT PHOTOGRAPHS
WITH TEXT BY RALPH NADING HILL

THE STEPHEN GREENE PRESS

BRATTLEBORO, VERMONT

in association with

Vermont Life Magazine and The Vermont Historical Society

ACKNOWLEDGMENTS: More than most books this is the work of many people, primarily of photographers, most of whom have long since gone to their rewards. They were social historians, whether they knew it or not, and we wish they could see their pictures in this album.

Second to thank are the generous librarians and other individuals who have let us use their photos, especially Charles T. Morrissey, Director of the Vermont Historical Society, T. D. S. Bassett and Connell Gallagher, Curator and Manuscript Librarian, respectively, of Special Collections, Bailey Library, University of Vermont. To part with original photographs for several weeks until they could be copied, required a good deal of faith on the part of the large number of people credited in the appendix (page 143).

Thirdly, a group that might be called the collators, who traveled around gathering the pictures (hundreds more than we finally selected), particularly Walter Hubbard, Deputy Director of the Vermont Historical Society, John R. Wood, who is responsible for a prodigious accumulation of facts about them, and Norman MacIver, who made copies of most of the photographs.

The design of the book and the matching of the photographs to the plan in which they are presented is the work of Linda Dean Paradee, Production Manager of *Vermont Life* magazine. Her contribution has been nothing short of invaluable.

Lastly the editors: Stephen Greene, who germinated the idea of a portfolio of historical photographs; Walter Hard, Jr., Editor Emeritus of *Vermont Life* magazine, who supervised it until his retirement, and Brian Vachon, Editor of *Vermont Life*, who finally coaxed the participants into action.

We hope all these individuals will consider the result equal to their exertions.
                                                                    —R.N.H.

The Vermont Bicentennial Commission is privileged to give its official endorsement to publication of *Vermont Album* as an outstanding contribution to proper commemoration of the Bicentennial. The Commission, however, has not expended public funds in the production of the book nor are any proceeds from its sale being used to support Commission programs.

This book is published by The Stephen Greene Press, Brattleboro, Vermont 05301 in association with Vermont Life Magazine, Montpelier, Vermont 05602 and The Vermont Historical Society, Montpelier, Vermont 05602. It has been produced in the United States of America: Composed by The Vermont Printing Company and printed and bound by The Colonial Press.

Library of Congress Cataloging in Publication Data

Hill, Ralph Nading, 1917-
    Vermont album.

    1. Vermont—Description and travel—Views.
2. Vermont—Social life and customs—Pictorial works.
I. Title.
F50.H52   778.9′9′9174303   74-13090
ISBN 0-8289-0218-6

        75 76 77 78 79 9 8 7 6 5 4 3 2

Contents

Dedicated to all citizens, native and imported, alive and departed,
who have shared the Vermont experience.

Vermont Album

How They Got There

BY 1839, when Louis Daguerre succeeded in capturing an image through a "camera obscura," Vermont had endured fourteen volcanic years as a republic and forty-eight as the Union's fourteenth state. The white man's encounter with the difficult country that became Vermont reaches further back almost seventeen decades if we include Samuel de Champlain's discovery of the lake and Green Mountains, the first French and English outposts and the French and Indian Wars.

All we know about the state's formative years is what we can glean from books, maps, journals, a few artifacts, and an occasional drawing or painting. We shall probably never know what Champlain or Ethan Allen looked like because no authentic likeness of either has ever appeared. The first-growth forests and the log cabin era of Revolutionary pioneers vanished almost without a trace. Fortunately the farms and valley hamlets changed little from the time they emerged from the wilderness until their images began to appear on glass plates. Except for larger towns and cities the face of the land indeed bore its traditional contours well into the twentieth century.

Photographs are the most truthful evidence we have of a nineteenth-century rural society. What surprises us about them are details we would otherwise have overlooked. A selection of old pictures may not tell the whole truth, but it is invaluable for its accumulation of overlooked details. The Daguerreotypes, glass plates, and stereopticon views, salvaged by libraries around the state, are an enlightening resource not only for historians, but also for critics of the Plastic Age who would recapture, if they could, the simplicity, stability, freedom and gemutlichkeit of those olden days. At least these are the qualities those unhurried decades, unencumbered with all the latest "improvements" and complications, seem to impart to the mind's eye.

If the camera's eye tells us anything about the last century it is that hard labor forged Vermont's home-made society. Except for the water wheel, people and animals were the sole sources of power, and their exertions were made even more strenuous by the state's vertical topography. Just getting from here to there required a prodigious expenditure of energy. Little wonder that early photographers seemed preoccupied with transportation. They took innumerable pictures of oxen, horses, sleighs, carriages, and stagecoaches, and they were entranced with that marvel of all time, the iron horse. Its arrival in the late 1840's was faithfully recorded, as were its frequent mishaps and occasional disasters; the local photographer could always be counted upon if the afternoon flyer jumped the track and plummeted down an embankment.

Equally useful, of course, was water-borne transport from the humble river ferry to the palatial side-wheel steamboat. In the 1880's came the horse car, soon to be replaced in the cities by the electric trolley, and finally the horseless carriage. Since no subject appears to have preoccupied Vermonters more deeply than transportation, a review is here presented, encompassing three-quarters of a century, of their quest for better ways to get there.

1

Since they seem to have no luggage, the destination of passengers on the roof of the "Addison House Bus," pausing in front of Middlebury hostelry, is presumably local. Opened in 1826 as the Vermont Hotel, on the site of a 1794 tavern which burned in 1816, Addison House had seen better days when this picture was taken in 1888. The Battell Block now occupies site. □ Two-man disaster squad with ax and rope (right) has cut through cakes of ice backed up by the West River on South Londonderry Road. Spring thaws still leave similar calling cards against bridges and back yards. Note off-center hitch enabling horses to follow track rather than navigate heavier snow in center ridge of the road.

2

3

People, horses, and rigs gather (left) in Sunday-best for the Fourth of July celebration in front of Canaan House in 1900; band is playing near porch. While not otherwise noted for swearing, Bill Buck, longtime owner of the hotel, usually ended his sentences with "By Jesus!" A number of his buggy whips had been stolen, and when a salesman taking an order for new ones asked what he wanted on the handles Bill replied: "Bill Buck, by Jesus!" When the whips were delivered that was what was printed on them. A few survive today. Typical, and architecturally pleasing with its many dormers and gables, Canaan House burned in 1930, was rebuilt, and burned again in 1936.

4

Man in buggy about to cross the Chiselville Bridge (above) was William F. Hayden, a professional photographer who lived on a farm north of the bridge in Sunderland and whose family is the seventh generation to occupy it. Photo was taken by Hayden's wife on their way home from a shopping trip to East Arlington. A nearby factory, run by water power from the Roar-ing Branch, for years made high-quality chisels, hence the name of the old bridge and a few houses clustered together in that Sunder-land community. Standing today, the much photographed Chiselville Bridge still has a good swimming hole below it enjoyed by area chil-dren. □ Below: When the Vernon Dam was built on the Connecticut, the Little River Bridge upstream in North Hinsdale had to be raised 10 feet with jacks placed on cribbing under each end. Before that the Connecticut and tributaries were often low enough in summer to cross by jumping from rock to rock. This wagon has been diverted across the dry bed of the Little River (which occasionally supplied stones for the crusher in Brattle-boro) during bridge alterations.

5

6

The heavily laden Concord Coach (above) stops at a hotel in South Londonderry. □ Station Agent Edward Willard (below, with derby) and Driver Wayne Yeaw pose on Williamsville-East Dover stagecoach, now in the Smithsonian Institution. Passengers, looking as if they had robbed a train, are actually railroad workers.

7

8

A traveler in south-central Vermont early in this century might have encountered Solon Underwood and wife out for a drive behind their ox, Bully. □ Below: Henry L. Sheldon, age 83, in the front seat, and S. W. Bidwell, 95, and Loyal L. Wright, 93, in back, appear in this 1903 Middlebury photo. The ancient carriage was used by President Monroe and Commodore Macdonough in Vermont. The flag flew with the Commodore at the Battle of Plattsburgh.

9

Freighted with Manchester children in front of Vermont's noted hotel, the Equinox "bus" also hauled guests from the railroad station in Manchester Center. Opening in 1853, the hotel evolved from Levi Orvis's spacious dwelling and store joined together. The railroad's arrival (1852) assured a growing supply of city people to rock on Equinox's ever-expanding piazza. □ A different kind of hostelry is shown below, with croquet on the lawn, and only a dirt road and telephone line to the outside world. Clientele came from railroad ads: "Mountain View Farm. Purchase ticket to West Townshend, and ask conductor to stop at Eddy's crossing. Accommodates 20. Terms $6 to $7 per week."

10

11

Vermont Central Railroad (later Central Vermont) was composed in southern Vermont of the Connecticut River R.R., reaching Brattleboro in 1849, and Vermont Valley R.R., completed to Bellows Falls in 1851. Main line here crossed the stone bridge built in 1878 over the mouth of Whetstone Brook, Brattleboro. Once a church in Guilford, the building behind engine was brought here and rebuilt about 1832, to become silk and grist mill and machine shop of John Gore, pioneer builder of a steam automobile. (Burned in 1888.) Beyond arch is the second Brattleboro House which was transformed into a hotel from the third of Jacob Estey's four organ factories. In front of the hotel is Main Street bridge. The rocks in the Connecticut River are now under water, backed up behind Vernon Dam. Bridge, camouflaged by a modern addition, still stands.

12

13

14

Woodstock Railroad's spectacular bridge over Quechee Gorge, 163 feet above the river, was built in 1875 by first erecting a spiderweb trestle and on top of it a closed-in lattice bridge 280 feet long. The 13.88-mile line from White River Junction to Woodstock opened that same year in August, beginning a struggling career of 58 years. Its most prosperous period was under the aegis of Frederic Billings of Royalton, President of the Northern Pacific R.R., who retired in Woodstock.

A self-propelled steam "inspection car" called *Gertie Buck* (now on display at Shelburne Museum), owned by the A. G. Dewey Company of Quechee, long served the Dewey family for junkets to White River Junction on the Woodstock line. Note carriage seats and mud guards.

Remarkable photo below shows a Missisquoi Valley R.R. wood-burning locomotive pulling into Sheldon Springs Station. Congress Hotel is at left. Hopefully the engine has stopped. If not, only seconds remain before the elderly couple seated on the platform are swept away by the cow-catcher.

15

Early wood burner with a vintage passenger car operated by the Boston, Concord, and Montreal Railroad stops on a two-deck wooden bridge over the Connecticut between Woodsville, N.H. and Wells River. First train crossed the bridge in May, 1853. Lower level served horse-drawn traffic. The Boston and Concord connected with the Connecticut and Passumpsic on Vermont side, and later became part of Boston and Maine. Abutments of the bridge can still be seen from a present iron highway bridge just to the south. The north-country is a graveyard of ambitious small lines striving to become lucrative connectors between Portland and Boston and the Great Lakes.

16

An ornate Central Vermont 4-4-0 American-type locomotive, *The Stranger*, built in October, 1852, emerges from the handsome four-portal St. Albans train shed, which was constructed in 1886-7 and was the last survivor of its type in the country. The 351-foot brick structure with curved roof cornices arching over its 88-foot ends served nearly a century as a major feature of C.V.'s station, shops, and office headquarters (background). Roof of the shed was supported by a series of arched wooden trusses of the Howe patent covered-bridge design.

17

18

Of the numerous calamities befalling early railroads, the collision of the engines *Vermont* (left) and *Sorelle* on May 20, 1864, must rank as among the most bizarre. It occurred one and a half miles north of St. Albans on the track of the Vermont and Canada (later Vermont Central). The *Vermont* was drawing an express train south from Rouses Point to connect with the steamboat line in Burlington; the northbound *Sorelle,* hauling freight cars laden with stone, had just left St. Albans. Seconds before the crash the engineer of the *Vermont* jumped, breaking his leg (but thereby saving his life), while the engineer of the *Sorelle* perished in his cab, crushed under the wheels of the *Vermont,* which had climbed up over it.

19

20

The worst railroad wreck in the history of Vermont, one which accelerated safety legislation throughout the country, occurred in the frigid darkness of February 5, 1887. Steaming through twenty-below-zero cold into a stiff north wind, the Montreal Express, having just left White River Junction, rounded the curve onto the 640-foot, four-span wooden trestle over the White River in Hartford. Suddenly the last cars jumped the track, and when the locomotive was half way across the bridge the engineer, having set the brakes,

looked back on a shocking scene: the Boston sleeper plummeting off the bridge, pulling the Springfield sleeper, the Springfield coach, and the Boston coach with it. The wooden cars disintegrated as they crashed onto the two-foot-thick ice of the river bed, their coal stoves and kerosene lamps setting them on fire and, in turn, the timbers of the bridge, which was totally consumed. Of the 90 passengers 34 died and 49 were injured. A defective rail on the curve leading to the bridge was found to have snapped in the extreme cold under the weight of the train. It had been made of unfinished Scottish steel and laid the same year it was rolled in St. Albans. The engineer was absolved of blame; the train had not been travelling at excessive speed. The death toll would have been far less had the cars been heated with steam and lighted by electricity, improvements adopted by many railroads not long thereafter. The picture of the charred remains by an unknown photographer (above left) was used for a drawing of the wreck in *Harper's Weekly;* photo (left) shows scene from a distance with a crowd of people on the ice, and on the embankment the lone baggage car which with locomotive and tender escaped destruction. So confident were the engineers of the durability of the new 650-foot iron bridge completed the year of the wreck that they tested it with twelve locomotives weighing 854 tons, and widely distributed the above picture, which served to reassure even the most dubious travelers.

22

The Rutland Railroad, for generations the mainstay of travel in western Vermont and after 1901 the shortest route between Montreal and New York, long served the city of Rutland as its principal industry. Early photo of the Rutland's bustling headquarters (above) shows a freight train, drawn by two 4-4-0 locomotives, before departure through the mountains on a branch line to Bellows Falls; train shed in right background over line to Troy, and the large dome (left) covering the turntable. □ Below: Rutland station in Vergennes with a Burlington-bound passenger train beyond. Circa 1900.

23

A ferry across the White River at Hartford, called *The Great Eastern*, after the 692-foot Atlantic steamship of same name, made as many as 170 trips a day from June through October of 1892 while townspeople were building the "first iron carriage bridge in town" to replace a condemned wooden span. A cable, running through sheaves and attached to each shore, kept the current from carrying the craft downstream. River ferries were propelled by "setting poles" pushed against bottom, by oars, or by sweeps eddying water in stern. Lake ferries employed almost every conceivable means of propulsion: sail, side wheels: horse-driven by way of treadmills on the deck, or by steam, and propeller.

Webber Ferry crossed the Connecticut at Putney. In 1829 the *Vermont*, a sternwheeler, penetrated the shoals of the Connecticut as far north as Brattleboro, and for a few years steamers no thicker than a sandwich, according to Charles Dickens who rode on one, ventured many miles further up to Wells River. But the northern Connecticut proved inhospitable and all attempts at navigating "heavy dew" ended.

24

25

Lake Champlain shipyard at Shelburne Harbor in the 1860's, showing the wrecks of two steamboats, with that of the *Francis Saltus* in the foreground. The steamer *R. W. Sherman* lies at the wharf, while the hull of the *Adirondack*, under construction, rests on the ways in the right background. In its famous competition against the old line, the *Saltus* (1844-1859) was involved in several desperate episodes. In one of them she was hijacked by a prize crew, brought to Shelburne Harbor, chained to a tree on shore and there defended by a judge who refused to be intimidated when her former crew appeared in a sloop and threatened him at gunpoint. Built in 1851, the very fast *Sherman* once raced from Port Kent to Burlington at twenty knots. Launched in 1867 the 251-foot *Adirondack* served only eight years. When she was dismantled her ornate stateroom hall went west to be built into the Great Lakes steamer, *City of Cleveland*, in 1880.

Three Lake Champlain steamboats bore the name *Vermont*. The first, launched in 1808, was the pioneer in regular service on any lake. The second, 272 feet in length, was launched in 1871. Carrying a crew of 60, she had 61 staterooms, President's and bridal suites, and a dining room for 150 people. Her 175-foot stateroom hall, constructed of 27 different kinds of wood garnished with gilded cupids' heads and oak leaves, was lighted with gas chandeliers. With a vertical beam engine fed by 1500-horsepower coal-burning boilers, she served, like her predecessors, on a line which ran the length of the lake, connecting in the north with trains to Montreal. The southern connection was with the steamers of Lake George and the Hudson River. It was a popular journey by inland river and lakes almost the whole distance between New York and Montreal. At left she passes Diamond Island. Below she rests in winter quarters at Shelburne Shipyard. After a long career she was retired in 1902.

27

28

The *Ticonderoga*, last of Champlain's fleet of 29 sidewheelers, built at Shelburne in 1906 (and now at the Shelburne Museum) is shown above at a temporary dock at Fort Crown Point during the 1909 Tercentenary Celebration of the discovery of the lake. During the ceremonies she carried President Taft and other notables. At right, seated on the forward promenade deck, are Vermont Governor George H. Prouty and staff. Back row, left to right: Maj. Aaron Grout, Mrs. Grout, Gov. Prouty, Col. J. E. Piddock, Gen. D. L. Morgan. Front row: Mrs. D. L. Noble, Mrs. Prouty, Mrs. C. E. Nelson, Mrs. J. E. Piddock.

View of Steamboat Wharf at Newport showing the Magog House, a fashionable "watering place" through the Civil War and Victorian eras. The steamers *Mountain Maid* (right), built in 1854 and *Lady of the Lake*, 1867, carried an international clientele, plying as they did Memphremagog's Canadian and American waters. □ The *Reindeer*, shown below at her Vergennes dock, was built in 1882 by the Grand Isle Steamboat Company. She ran between Burlington and St. Albans and served as an excursion boat for the Central Vermont Railroad, calling at every Champlain port including Vergennes, eight miles up the Otter Creek, where she had just enough room to warp her 180 feet around in the basin below the falls.

31

32

33

Most of Vermont's many small lakes had their pickerel-shaped naphtha launches which burned a colorless oil distillate, thus saving their passengers from the dusting of a coal-burning launch. The *Little Nellie* (also shown moored in front of the *Vermont II* on page 25) ran a ferry service between Vergennes and Westport, also carried "parties of pleasure." Private steam launches were ultimate status symbols for affluent Vermonters. □ Below: the Burlington family of William Wells, a Civil War general, out for a cruise. The hole in the roof had to be of ample size to prevent the hot smokestack from setting the canopy on fire.

34

35

36

37

The Shaftsbury lady on the bicycle is Mary Monroe Hawkins, a school teacher who "boarded around," also the only woman telegrapher and railroad station agent in Vermont at that time (circa 1895). Lady with crutches, Irene Canfield, did not fall off the bicycle, but had arthritis. Ida Parsons, her sister, stands behind her. Man behind bicycle is Wallace White; young man at right is Ernest, son of Irene. □ Left: great conclave of cyclists in Woodstock during Gilded Age. Buildings are much the same today except for the roof over sidewalk in front of Prior Brothers' furniture store, the ornate watering trough in the street, and the gas lights beyond.

38

A "pyrotechnical display," Chinese lanterns along the right of way, Sherman's Military Band, and the Westford Drum Corps celebrated the completion of Burlington's horse car railroad in November, 1885. Following the principal streets, with a branch across the river to Winooski, the line served depot, fairgrounds, and opera house, with arrangements for "theatre cars" to stand in readiness outside after each entertainment. Twenty-five horses operated the railroad. After several derailments the tracks were relaid around curves. In December, stoves were installed in the closed cars. A month after it was completed, high water swept away the bridge to Winooski. The narrow gauge tracks proved too narrow and later had to be widened. Other than that the line functioned well enough until it was electrified in 1893. Presumably photographed when open cars replaced closed ones in the summer of 1886, the dignitaries above were (left to right) W. H. Hendee, K. B. Walker, J. D. Hatch, A. E. Richardson, Louis Turk, Elias Lyman, and Joseph Lepp, "motorman."

Service on the six-and-a-half-mile trolley line (right) between Bellows Falls and Saxtons River began in 1900. A chief destination was Barber Park midway between the two towns. When it opened each summer a trolley with a brass band toured the two towns. □ Below: a three-car baseball special heads for the park in St. Albans. Line opened in 1900, and was extended to Swanton in 1902. A branch to St. Albans Bay carried railroad excursionists from the Central Vermont depot in town to the steamboat dock at the Bay.

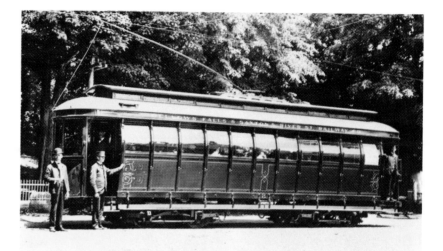

39

40

45

46

Racing the train could be a hazardous pastime, particularly where the road kept crossing the railroad tracks, as did old Route 30 east of West Townshend. The troubled West River R.R. has long been defunct and the above terrain is now under water behind a flood control dam. □ Left: Drivers of an early Glidden Tour gather at Kendrick's Hotel in Putney to compare notes on blowouts, engine failures, and directions to next rendezvous. Automobile Blue Book was the motorists' bible: "Where poles turn left just beyond watering trough, keep straight ahead. Cross iron bridge, passing bandstand on right, bear left at reverse fork beyond blacksmith shop, then right at cemetery and up steep hill. Caution—sharp right and left down steep grade to irregular four corners. Bear left at white house with red barn. Hilly and sandy road thru woods."

It's time out for Moxie at the Bradford Fair. The top of the two-chair convertible is prevented from blowing off by guy straps attached near springs; brass stays on the adjustable windshield accomplished the same purpose. □ Below: Highlight of the day for the family of O. R. Wright at River View Farm (Box 43) in Newfane is dispensing mail from the postman's typical leather pouch. Though mud-covered windshield has no wiper, the Model N's right-hand drive at least enables postman to put the mail in the box without leaving his seat—which is more than can be said for modern RFD vehicles. Restfulness of this scene is augmented by rope hammocks fastened to trees behind the lady in rocker.

47

48

49

East Proctor road to Rutland with abandoned touring car speaks volumes for pre-macadam conditions in 1913 when this photo was taken. Other than for the quality of its roads Proctor had already become a model mining community—without a saloon in town. Exception that proved rule was story of tipsy miner who joined in the singing with a Rutland Salvation Army group. When the leader asked him if he would like to work for the Lord, he replied: "Oh no, I have a good job in Proctor."

This auto-buggy collision occurred near Bellows Falls, in 1916. Man in the buggy (left) was "Chan" Beebe, farmer and peddler of "hulled corn 'n' hominy," who lived a short distance from scene. After the accident the horse drawing damaged wagon broke loose and ran into a Bellows Falls trolley a mile away in Gageville, injuring two men and fatally injuring the horse. The horse at right was brought in to remove the wagon by the young man, presumably Ruel K. Thayer. □ 1911 photo in Montpelier (below) at rear of Lawrence block (which remains nearly the same today) shows Frank Towne, "son of Harry Towne of Towne Hill," with his oxen extricating a car from some problem or other. Passengers in car (Harry Rivers holds up license plate) appear in good spirits—suggesting they had gone in for a beer until help arrived.

50

51

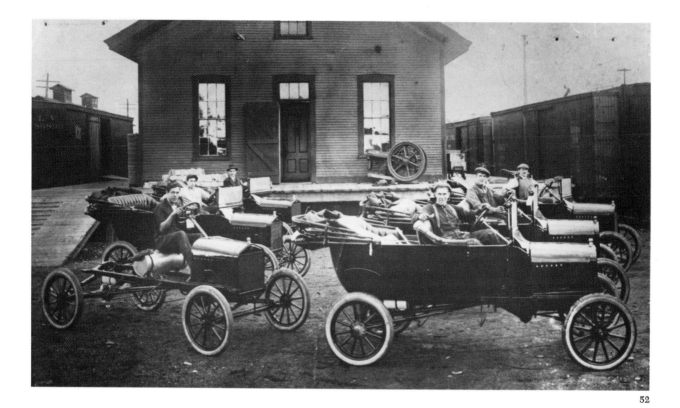

52

Assembling new Fords which had arrived in freight cars in pieces was a familiar activity at the Middlebury depot. Above Model T's, all same model and all black, appear to have been shipped without running boards and fenders, and car at left without body or windshield. Even so, the man seated on the gas tank could drive it away and pick up parts on next shipment. □ Below: Sidewheeler *Chateaugay*, with much of her main deck stripped of superstructure for ferrying cars, awaits a bumper crop on Burlington pier. By the late 'twenties the number of carriages and wagons (left center) had dwindled. A century-and-a-half of ferry service across Lake Champlain to Port Kent, N.Y., Ausable Chasm, and Adirondacks continues today.

53

54

Vermont's last experiment in building automobiles was the elegant Wasp, manufactured in several classic models by Karl Martin, auto designer and coach craftsman on Pleasant Street in Bennington after World War I. After designing the popular Roamer in 1916 and a stint in Naval aviation, Martin arrived in Bennington in 1919. Two years later he produced the handsome phaeton above. With its many original features it created a sensation in the Commodore Hotel lobby during the New York automobile show. Its sharply pointed fenders jutted straight out giving the car a dignified yet dashing profile. The finest craftsmanship was apparent down to the headlights and hair cloth rugs. Although the Wasp was capable of 70 MPH with its four cylinder engine, Martin added a six on a larger chassis in 1924. Unfortunately that was the next to last year he made cars in this 26-man shop. But in the few years he had made the Wasp (18 in all) his designs and workmanship made history, proving once again, as if proof were needed, that good things are rare and come slowly, and that quality does not usually mix with mass production.

"VERMONT," wrote Ira Allen in his history, "contains everything within itself that can contribute to the immediate wants, convenience, and even luxury of man." He spoke of the climate as "friendly to population and longevity, notwithstanding it partakes of heat and cold in high degrees which gradually make their approaches."

He described rivers and lakes full of fish and nature not less bountiful in fowl and quadrupeds; lands well calculated for agriculture, abounding also in iron ore, copper, limestone, clay, and marble; and forests full

What They Did

of various species of timber—in short an alluring country well suited to the aspirations of settlers. He acknowledged that the winter cold had been known to reach minus twenty-seven. He recorded the average depth of snow; he did not mention that all that could be done with it was to roll it, or with ice, to cut it. He showed, withall, remarkable prescience as to what people in Vermont would be doing.

Whatever other resources might be harvested under, on, or above the ground, none compared with Kings' ransoms of white pine—some 150 feet tall and eight feet across the butt—growing in lordly profusion from border to border. What might be called the Age of Wood was indeed inaugurated by the broadaxes of George III felling mast pines for the Royal Navy. Each spring for well over a century a freshet of logs tumbled down our rivers—an avalanche of wood moving down the Connecticut with such inexorable force that it sometimes swept bridges before it. Bound together in rafts, millions of board feet were floated north and south out of Lake Champlain to Canada and New York. To generations of Vermonters wood was the ultimate provider. They built their farms and towns, their implements and conveyances with it; they burned it to keep warm, they tapped it for sugar.

After the wood had been harvested there remained the land, which produced everything they ate and wore. Nature compensated for its harsh winter with a lush growing season, and Vermonters experimented with every crop and animal that could sustain their remote, self-sufficient world. For a long time they did very well with sheep. The dairy cow never failed to justify her place of honor on the state seal. More than dominate the landscape, she largely created it. Even the small town, the butcher, baker and candlestick maker owed her their presence.

Other than the marble which Ira Allen reported, and granite and slate which he did not, Vermont's rocks proved anything but salable, though there was plenty of clay for the local brickyard and enough copper and other minerals for a few mines. Vermont's most distinctive natural resource therefore became natural resourcefulness. To characterize its economy as strictly rural, even from the start, would be to ignore the castle-builders in their drafty sheds, out of which sprang platform scales, machine tools, and parlor organs, and such lively towns to produce them as St. Johnsbury, Springfield, and Brattleboro.

Nor could Allen, writing in the 1790's, have divined that the "hills and mountains with many beautiful and productive valleys" and "extensive fine plains and meadows" would for their charm alone become Meccas for weary city dwellers. Well before the Civil War, a springtide of watering places and hotels overspread the landscape. Most difficult of all for Allen to have prophesied was our worthiest resource and prime export—seemingly the offspring of climate and environment—a special breed of vigorous, durable, ingenious, practical, and, as Sinclair Lewis branded them, "cautiously humorous" people.

55

56

In winter, farmers had the time and horsepower to work in their woodlots, which were much more accessible by sled. Frank Bell, Sr. (with the beard in the background above), a Scot whose thick burr was quite at home in Vermont which had an early Scottish settlement, ran the logging job on the Royal Cole farm on Kemp Hill in Canaan about 1904. The woman in the shawl was his wife and the two younger women, unaccountably in their Sunday best, were his daughters. The children belonged to Frank Bell, Jr., in the foreground holding the ax. □ A Mr. Jelly (left) had to haul his logs 12½ miles to Willard's mill in Townshend. On the return trip he would erect a blanket tepee on the empty sled and put the hot stove and himself in it. The oxen presumably knew the way as he journeyed home in comfort.

57

Of the various ways of getting logs to the mill the "log chute" at Grafton (above left) seems the most dubious, at least in this 1905 photo. Filled with water from some mysterious source at the top of the hill, the chute sluiced the logs down into the foreground to be hauled to the mill. (If the top of the chute had as many leaks as the bottom, the logs must have arrived spasmodically, and thoroughly dry.) ☐ The striking picture at right (circa 1912) of the White River choked with logs behind the dam in Sharon shows four piers (far left) which, connected by a boom of chains, held back the logs until they were all collected. They

were then pushed over the dam, floated to the Connecticut and from there south to Massachusetts or even Long Island Sound. The steam-driven sawmill on the shore was a local operation which had nothing to do with the drive. ☐ Right: The great drive of 1914 has just passed the junction of the White and Connecticut rivers, and the horse rafts are pulling stranded logs off the banks and shoals. Other rafts carry hay and grain for the horses, a blacksmith, his forge and anvil, and dry wood for the kitchen stove. The cook scow stands ready to stoke the voracious appetites of the loggers, also those of local children, with its famous baked bean

and flapjack suppers. When teams loaded with hawsers, tents, and supplies passed through river towns the people knew the drive wasn't far behind. As the great horizontal forest moved downriver the drivers expertly applied pressure to "key" logs to prevent jams from forming. The small boat with the pointed prow beyond the cook scow was called a bateau, which could be skillfully maneuvered in expert hands. In the drive of 1914–15 two thousand lumbermen in the woods around the headwaters of the Second Connecticut Lake cut some 40 million feet of timber, requiring a 500-man crew for the drive. The last great stand of white

58

pine was cut at Concord in 1920. Before 1890 oxen, less susceptible to sickness and surer-footed in snow and mud, were used to haul big logs out of the woods to the riverbank. But they are also exceedingly slow and were ultimately replaced by horses. After the last big logs had gone downriver, pulpwood followed. The worst bottleneck was Bellows Falls, where getting the logs over the dam consumed three to six weeks. The long annals of the drives, which began in the northeast and migrated west, supplied the river towns with a good deal of folklore—and the language with such words as "logjam" and "haywire."

59

60

Combination shingle, saw, and gristmill long stood in English Mills, later called Prosper, a small settlement north of Woodstock. Named after their owner, Joel English (1766-1852), the mills were enlarged about 1889, some 11 years before the above photo was taken. Sign standing at right of door, flanked by millstones, reads: "Sawdust sold at this mill at one cent per bushel & pay for the same when you get it." View at right is of interior of the mill. The man and curly-headed little girl, whittling, who couldn't quite sit still for the camera, are unknown.

61

During the latter part of the nineteenth century some of the wood used by Lake Champlain mills came through the canal from the St. Lawrence on barges, hauled up the lake by steam tugs. The picture below was taken in the basin at Vergennes, where wood for the shade roller plant is being unloaded. Bargemen's living quarters were in little houses in the stern.

62

63

The lumbering operation known as the "Bronson Job," run in Sunderland at the turn of the century by Silas Giffith of Danby, included a blacksmith shop, general store, boarding house, and school. From about April to August the men sawed the 50-to-60-foot logs they had sledded to the mill, whose steam engine was driven by a boiler burning chips and slabs. What sawdust they couldn't burn was blown into a nearby stream, killing the fish all the way down to East Arlington. The barrels on the roof were kept full of water in the event that sparks from the smokestacks settled on the shingles. □ Another method of cutting wood was the "horse power" (right), homemade or bought from a manufacturer. Models operated by goats for separating milk were also available.

64

65

Other than lumbering, no regimen exceeded ice-cutting in foot-pounds of energy expended. The two men at left are laying up a supply at Ashton Timson's in Williamsville in 1909. Two generations have grown up without knowing the routine of the iceman with his tongs hoisting a cake over the leather apron on his shoulder and sliding it into the ice box; the pleasure of jumping on the ice wagon and cutting off a piece; or, on a blistering summer day, the fragrant coolness of the sawdust in the local ice house. The scene below is in North Calais.

66

No activity is more indigenous to Vermont than sugaring. The bounty of the rock maple was well known to the Indians, who notched the trees with their stone axes, inserted wooden spouts, and made syrup by dropping hot stones into troughs of sap. Early photos of wooden tubs of sap hauled by oxen, and of outdoor boiling in large iron kettles demonstrate that sugaring remained a primitive process until well into this century when the above photo was taken in northwestern Vermont. The farmer has obviously made the sled and probably the collecting tub. To save steps he has constructed a trough to carry the sap emptied with the bucket from the big tub to a holding tank, from which another trough runs to the evaporator inside his sugar house. □ Below: The Canaan sugaring-off party would probably have had sugar-on-snow, but since it is too warm for that they are sampling freshly made syrup in dishes—except for the man in the derby who is supplying his needs from a pail.

69

The absence of every trapping of the abundant life invests this poignant scene with a suggestion of what is missing in an affluent society. In the face of bare subsistence on a Bridgewater hilltop the farmer's son has spent days or weeks building his wagon, all the way down to the wooden flanges holding the home-made wheels on to what appear to be home-made wooden axles; and no doubt just as long trying to persuade the sheep to pull it. But what fun when he succeeded—a kind of fun peculiarly unresponsive to the elaborateness of one's possessions or diversions. The scene has, to be sure, a melancholy starkness about it, yet everything is relative. The boy may never have seen a town larger than Bridgewater, but the world he knew and cared about was the world of these hills.

Thirteen decades ago some two-and-a-quarter million sheep grazed on Vermont hillsides, many of them offspring of the merinos brought from Spain by the American minister at Madrid, William Jarvis of Weathersfield. Offers of $10,000 were refused for the best prize rams. As sheep-raising migrated west after the Civil War, Vermont flocks began to dwindle until in the first third of this century a few head here and there, as above in Georgia, were all that remained. □ Getting the hay in remains as critical as ever for Vermont dairymen but the haystack, the team, wagon, and pitchfork have all but vanished from the fields. Below: The Frank Guindon farm in Lincoln with Mount Abraham in the background.

72

The tranquil scene near Randolph (left) was one of the many in the neighborhood photographed after the turn of the century by two sisters, Grace and Nell Conant. □ Right: The grandmother of Harriet Fisher of Lyndonville feeds her flock in front of a barn well stocked with fire wood on the Fletcher farm. □ George Davis, shown below feeding his White Brahmas during the 1890's, was born in this house on the Quaker Willow Farm in East Montpelier, lived there all his life, and died there in 1910. The house with its typical narrow clapboards, the center addition with somewhat wider ones, and the barn presumably tacked on later, compose a modest example of the "continuous" architecture characteristic of old Vermont farms. Note bird cage hanging in front door.

73

74

Strawberry picking on the Fred McNeil farm in New Haven about 1898. H. B. Slack, seated with his family in the surrey, owner of a market in Vergennes, bought strawberries from the McNeils, whose farm buildings in the background are no longer standing. ☐ Below:

Thrifty fields of tobacco in Putney in the heart of "Cigar Valley" on the Connecticut for years brought good returns to farmers who were willing to cope with frost, hail, worms, and monopoly buyers (the worms were the easiest to deal with) in the raising of Vermont's

unlikeliest crop. For several years early in the century the state ranked first in tobacco yield per acre, though growing it proved so risky not many acres were planted. Leaves were used for cigar wrappers and binders.

The hired man, seated on a crate of Plymouth Rock hens, turns the grindstone while George Boyce sharpens the cutting knives on his Worcester Branch road farm near Montpelier about 1902. Boyce's grandson looks up from his edifice of corncobs with rapt attention. The overhead bucket supplies water for the grindstone. The lady in the poster advertises the Stevens Leader 5¢ cigar. □ Below: Reaping time in Pike's meadow in Berlin about 1913.

77

78

79

When Vermont sheep-raising succumbed to cheaper western wool the farmers turned to the cow, not to milk (which was too perishable in the early days to ship out in any great quantity) but to its by-products: nine million pounds of cheese in 1849, and thirty years later 25 million five-pound crocks of butter. With rapid transportation by rail to the Boston-New York market the production of milk, 200 gallons for each inhabitant by 1890, became the principal occupation of Vermont farmers—which it remains today. Though thousands of 50-cow hill farms are growing up to timber, those in the river valleys as in Richmond (above) and in the lowlands of the Champlain basin are bigger than ever. □ The outdoor milking parlor at right appeared with no local identification on an old Vermont postcard, on the back of which the anonymous donor wrote: "I don't know if you care for this old shot but will send it along anyway."

80

The local creamery, a casualty of long-distance transport by refrigerated truck, often competed with the country store as a favorite gathering place. The Elgin Spring Creamery (above), operated by Fred Sears on Route 22 in Panton, burned in 1920 and was rebuilt in a new location west of Addison Corners. The damp, pungent clattering of the creamery, along with that of the cider mill, are indelible recollections.

81

82

Edmund Burke raised cows, pigs, horses, chickens, and six children on his 90-acre South Royalton farm. After he had stuck and bled a hog he placed it in a boiling cauldron over an outdoor fire to soften the bristles which he "shaved" off with a pair of old tin candlesticks. Then he cut it up into roasts which he packed in ice and covered with sawdust, and hams and bacons which he pickled in brine and smoked over a corncob fire. He pickled the feet, used the head to make head cheese, and "tried out" or melted down the fat into lard, which he pressed into blocks and wrapped in cheese cloth, for use as shortening, in frying, and as a lubricant. Burke and his family did all the work on his farm and some at his neighbors' when they needed it, and vice-versa—which was called "changing work." He was also a good hand at barn raisings and in doing anything else that he had a mind to. He lived from 1846 to 1915.

Until well into the twentieth century many people did not bring home the bacon; it was brought to them in the meat wagon. Heavily stocked at the market, the wagon served a list of customers on a regular route, the butcher cutting the meat on the tail gate. On Thursday the wagons often carried only fish. At right John Lewis, knife in hand in 1909, delivers meat at the South Newfane store.

83

An elaborately decorated wagon loaded with trunks of merchandise to be sold to stores wholesale stops in front of L. L. Dutcher's in St. Albans. Note the double-headed eagle on the roof. □ Below: dry goods were distributed the same way, the proprietors of city emporiums often holding "coat and suit openings" in smaller country stores.

84

Below: Prior to 1900 bales of rags reached the John Slack shoddy mill in Springfield by team, as did everything else before construction of the electric railway connecting with the main line of the Central Vermont. The Springfield mill employed 1200 Russians who maintained their own Orthodox Church.

85

86

William H. Williams of Williamsville, the first of four generations to run the above store, built it in 1828 as a sideline to a nearby wool and carding mill, where he had been "bound out" when very young as an expert dyer of scarlet cloth. He eventually bought the mill, taking advantage of its water power to add millstones for grinding corn and wheat. Although the mill eventually fell victim to changing conditions, the store (and post office) was just getting its second wind in the hands of Hastings Williams a century later. ☐ Below: In 1909 the indefatigable Porter Thayer photographed J. A. Davis and his wife in their West Dover general store, still being used today as the post office. Davis also sold meat and grain and served as the local purchasing agent for a St. Johnsbury maple sugar firm.

The last post office in the town of Searsburg was run in the shack at right by Needham Drury Bartlett (standing in doorway), a vegetarian with a profound knowledge of the Bible. Nearby on a terraced hillside he raised tomatoes, cucumbers, beans, and peas, spurning all ground-covered vegetables which he claimed were fit only for beasts. A visitor to the post office could call him from his garden by pulling a cord next to the door which led up the hill to a length of stove pipe in which was suspended a can filled with gravel. If he wasn't in his garden, a system of interchangeable signs such as "Call at woodshed" announced his whereabouts. The post office, with its two-drawered thread case, one for first- and the other for second-class mail, occupied half of the 12-by-20-foot shack and paid Bartlett $72 to $90 a year depending on business. A couch, rocking chair, cook stove, and bench took up the rest of the floor space. The walls were lined with shelves of patent medicines, old magazines, and miscellaneous other items which Bartlett occasionally sold. He also edited the *Christian Citizen*, a monthly which rarely appeared on time. Searsburg once boasted several schools, a hotel, and a larger combined post office and stagecoach station, its population of 235 supported by

89

tanneries, lumber mills, and woodworking industries making washboards, tables, and bedsteads. But the town gradually went downhill and when Bartlett died at the age of 84 in 1933 that was the end of the post office and the *Christian Citizen*, if not quite the end of Searsburg. □ Below: Lounging area was

the main feature of the sparsely stocked general store at Damon's Crossing in Victory in the heart of the Northeast Kingdom. A branch of the St. Johnsbury and Lake Champlain Railroad, long since abandoned along with the store, served the Moose River Lumber Co. operation in the Victory bog.

90

UNDERTAKERS [AND DEALERS IN] FURNITURE

91

Not long ago an out-of-stater stopped to ask a farmer why Vermont has so many cemeteries. "Because," he answered, "people have been dyin' here longer." It might also be added that they used to die more often—of tuberculosis, diphtheria, typhoid, and scarlet fever. The lugubrious building above with its forthright sign was, as it indicates, the property of M. V. Hicks, a Fairfax undertaker who augmented his line of furniture, caskets, and rough boxes with wagons, harnesses and whips. Combination furniture stores and funeral parlors (or "homes," in deference to the modern euphemism) were not the least unusual. The horses at left delivered freight to the store from the railroad. The white team, used for funerals, was skittish, and once deposited its cargo in pieces on to the porch of the local drugstore. Hicks, it is said, "was a compassionate man, and after the death of a townsman was heard to remark, with tears running down his cheeks: 'It's too bad he had to go, but we need the money.'" The building now houses the Fairfax fire department.

92

The problem of mining, cutting and transporting as hard and heavy a stone as granite precluded its use (with a few exceptions like the State House) as a building stone. The livelihood of the many companies who have mined it and the army of men who arrived to cut and finish it have therefore depended upon memorials and monuments, as the Barre Guild prefers to call them. Though the huge geometric pits on Millstone Hill have been growing rapidly deeper during the last century, the supply is almost inexhaustible. The building in 1890 of the hill-climbing Barre and Chelsea Railroad, connecting with the Central Vermont at Montpelier Junction, solved Millstone Hill's pressing transportation problem. Early view below looks southwest from the present Wells and Lamson quarry.

93

94

Isaac Underhill opened America's first marble quarry in Dorset in 1785. For decades dependence upon hand and water power severely limited Vermont's output. The advent of the gang-saw (enabling slabs to be cut into rectangular blocks) and of pneumatic drills and polishing machines fostered a major industry dominated by the Vermont Marble Company in Proctor, which acquired far-flung interests in other marble-producing countries. Open pits such as that above and underground penetrations 350 feet deep have produced marble for most cities—1,000 carloads for the Washington, D.C., Supreme Court building alone. As in Barre, artisans from Italy were imported to create designs called for in monumental buildings. The man at right uses a pneumatic drill, but his mallet and chisel for the finer work are handy nearby.

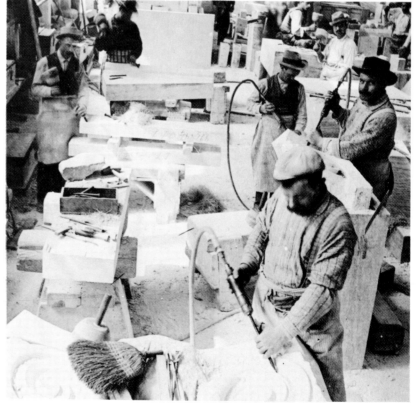

95

The name of the town had been changed from Vershire to Ely though no honor or credit was due the owner of its copper mine, Smith Ely, who extracted from the ore and the laborers every dollar he could, while his grandson paraded around town with diamonds on his fingers. Behind two months in their wages, the miners struck in July 1883 and cleaned out the company store. The press, local and metropolitan, was alarmed, for strikes in those days were synonymous with anarchy. Although the men had gone to Ely's house with the intention of hanging him, General Steven Thomas had talked them out of any violence, and there was none. The distraught faces of the miners' wives appearing in their smudgy windows were the only sign of life as the national guard marched into the town's single street. There was no resistance, no insolence, not even discourtesy on the part of the laborers, unless the remark of one of them, when asked if he were a miner, could be interpreted as such. "No sorr. I am at prisint a gentleman of indepindint laysure." Governor John Barstow ordered the company's tills emptied of every dollar in order to pay the miners $4,000 in back wages. The rest due them, $16,000, was to be paid in installments, but the company was in such poor condition that many of them wandered away without ever receiving it.

96

97

98

The carriage factory near the Burlington waterfront, operated by Charles Gray and Son from about 1850 to 1885, still stands. □ Left: Founded in Brandon in 1857 by John Howe (who bought the patent for a platform scale operated by ball bearings from its inventor, Frank M. Strong of Vergennes) the Howe Scale Company was later moved to its present location in Rutland, where it has since developed scales big enough to weigh the largest airplane. The original platform scale, balanced on knife edges (the invention of Thaddeus Fairbanks of St. Johnsbury), became the foundation of the sprawling Fairbanks Morse Corporation. By the mid-twentieth century, St. Johnsbury and Rutland were supplying nearly three-quarters of the nation's scales.

Founded by the family of General William Wells, last commander of the Army of the Potomac, Wells Richardson & Co. in Burlington made Paine's Celery Compound, "a Vermont Medicine that has the largest sale of any medicine in the world." Mixed in huge vats and shipped out by the carload, this nostrum with its high alcoholic content at least made its patrons feel better (temporarily) even though it did not improve their health. Extolled as its virtues were, on posters in covered bridges throughout the country, Paine's Celery Compound made a large fortune for the Wells family but ran afoul of the Pure Food and Drug Act of the twenties. □ Below: The Dan G. Spaulding brickyard at Taftsville showing part of the horse-operated "grinder" for mixing the clay, found nearby on the Spaulding farm, with the fine sand from the riverbank of the Ottauquechee. After they were molded, the bricks had to dry for two weeks in the yard before going to the kiln.

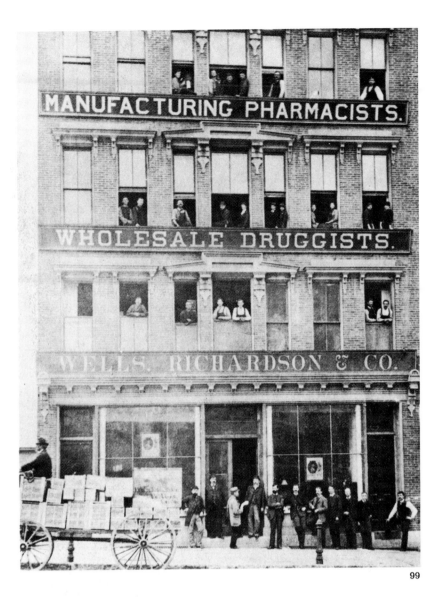

99

100

101

Whether the piano company, below the falls of the Black River in Springfield, made pianos or served as a wholesaler or retailer remains unfathomable by local historians. This much is known: the bridge here was built in the square and hauled across the river in one piece by a derrick. Circa 1870.

The Estey Organ Company in Brattleboro, at one time the world's largest maker of reed and pipe organs, was established by Jacob Estey, who started out as a plumber and manufacturer of lead pipe. In the early days he loaded up wagons with melodeons and peddled them around New England himself. Outgrowing several plants, the company finally moved to the complex of buildings shown below, housing the entire process from lumber yard to sales rooms. Although no longer in business, Estey was long a household word, providing the parlors of the world with some half a million reed instruments, and church lofts with several thousand pipe organs.

102

103

Even as late as 1883, when the above barn was erected on Bay View Farm near Long Point in Ferrisburg, local builders were still building them the old way, without a single nail in the frame. The beams were shaped with broad axes, adzes, and chisels and the mortised joints were locked with wooden pegs. Seventy feet long, 70 feet high, and 45 feet wide, this barn and many others like it were designed to carry slate roofs weighing four tons, as well as periodic heavy snowfalls. Native slate, which until several decades ago was cheap and plentiful, must be credited with the survival of this structure and many others much earlier in prime condition. A stone cistern for watering stock is seen in the forward end of the ground floor. □ Right: Tradesmen gather in front of their handiwork: the Williamstown Congregational Church, built in 1904.

104

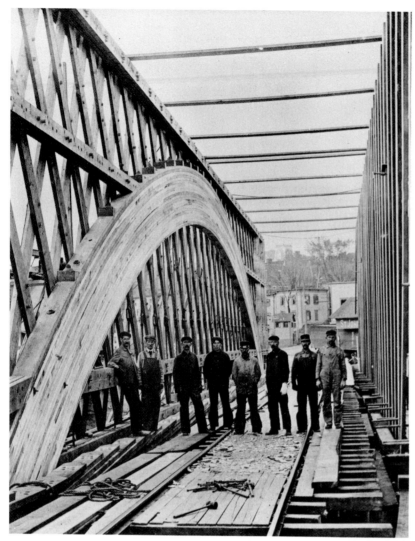

Wooden bridge built by the Maine Central Railroad spanned the Passumpsic River at St. Johnsbury until it was damaged in the flood of 1927 when two other bridges floating downriver came to rest against it. Note laminated arch performing the same function as large handhewn timbers of earlier bridges. Roof was added last. Steel bridge replacing this one still crosses the river near Portland Street.

105

Coffer dam for New England Electric System's first hydroelectric plant on the Connecticut at Vernon in 1907. Bulkheads of rock and timber permitted pumping water out of the basin so that cement foundations of the dam could be poured. Upon completion of this section, the same process was repeated on the far side of the river. Dam-building of one kind or another on all rivers large and small was a primary occupation throughout the nineteenth century.

106

During the early 1800's, all able-bodied men were required to work out their taxes in labor on the town roads. Later they had the choice of paying or working. By the time Porter Thayer photographed the men above, scraping Lock Hale Road between South Newfane and Williamsville, they were employees of the town. □ The coldest job in the world, according to those who did it, was rolling snow on the main roads after heavy storms—for it was then easier by far to pack than remove.

109

110

We are so accustomed to seeing *old* blacksmiths (since until recently, at least, they were all that remained) that the authenticity of the above photo of the Williamstown blacksmith shop in the early 1900's somehow seems questionable. □ Below: Joe Page, harness maker and cobbler in his Grafton shop. Strips of leather inserted into the top of the leather vise (right near window) were held firm by the spring action of its two arms. Vermont cobblers often traveled from farm to farm making shoes for the whole family (frequently from leather they had tanned), one wooden last or pattern for each member serving both left and right feet.

The well from which Olive Hanks drew water in South Randolph five or six decades ago symbolized that a farm woman's work was never done. A stone or heavy object attached to the other end of the long sweep at least made the task of raising a bucketful of water from a deep well less burdensome. □ Weaving palm-leaf hats was an important activity up and down Windham County's West River valley around the turn of the century. The leaves were distributed to housewives and the hats picked up on another trip. J. H. Fullerton of West Townshend was reported as furnishing leaves to some 2000 persons who braided 15 to 20 thousand hats for him a year.

111

112

Nothing so graphically characterized the self-sufficient Vermont homestead as the spinning wheel. Mrs. Bingham of South Newfane is shown with hers in 1916. □ "Setting," a favorite pastime particularly during the long winter months, is demonstrated by Mr. and Mrs. Sherb Moore in their Barnet living room early in the 1900's.

113

114

The last panther, or "catamount" as it was traditionally called, was shot in Barnard in 1881 by Alexander Crowell, shown at right with his trophy against a photographer's backdrop. Long exhibited in the museum of the Vermont Historical Society, it became rather peaked, and was recently refurbished for future generations.

115

116

117

A proud Middlebury hunting party of seven men and six dogs are shown with 23 trophies that the Pierce House chef appears ready to commit to his oven and table. Left to right: Hub Potter, Jim Smith, Harry Williams, Ed Daniels, John Higgins, Dewitt Walch, Cushing Hill, and Arthur Coffin. □ The bear is the subject of the following testimony of Porter Thayer who photographed it with Jim Mundell in 1913: "Jim was chopping wood with his favorite dog nearby when a big black bear walking on a ledge above them lost his footing and tumbled down near man and dog. The dog started to bark with fear and the bear commenced to chase the dog around the tree. Old Jim thought a lot of that dog so he waited until he got a good chance and then killed the bear with one whack of his axe."

Considering the Revolution, the War of 1812, the Civil War, and five wars in the last century, Vermont has done its share of fighting. It lost more men in the Civil War in proportion to its population than any other state. At left the Third Vermont Regiment is shown in St. Johnsbury on July 20, 1861 just before its departure on a train of 22 cars. The humanity of Abraham Lincoln forever immortalized a private of this regiment, William Scott of Company K, who was condemned to death for falling asleep on picket duty, after the same duty the two previous nights when he substituted for a sick comrade. The night before the execution the President telegraphed an order that it be stayed, but fearing it might not reach its destination in time he drove ten miles in his carriage to deliver it in person. A few months later the twenty-two-year-old Scott was killed while charging Confederate rifle pits at Lee's Mills.

118

On October 19, 1864 at three in the afternoon a detachment of 22 Confederate soldiers raided the banks of St. Albans from Canada and, with the town virtually defenseless, galloped back across the border with $208,000. Half of them, carrying $80,000 of the total, were caught. Six of these are shown at right prior to their trial, with the commander of the expedition, Lt. Bennett H. Young, at far right. He testified that the parting words of the Secretary of War for the Confederate States had been: "Lieutenant, you go upon a dangerous mission, and you and your command shall be fully protected." And so they were—by the Canadian courts, which released them together with their loot, holding that acts of war are just such acts as belligerents choose to commit within the territories of each other, whether or not launched from a neutral country.

119

Canada, part of an empire that favored the South, was anything but neutral, and the decision of its courts to free the St. Albans raiders (even though the Canadian government eventually paid Vermont the equivalent of the $80,000 it had released to them) stirred up great resentment in the Green Mountain State, adding to the rancor that had been festering for other reasons since the War of 1812. A group which banded together as the Fenians, the Irish who had immigrated to the United States after the potato famine of 1846–7, found Vermonters sympathetic to their schemes for redress against the British by striking at Canada. The movement, apparent at various points along the border as far west as St. Paul, Minnesota, culminated in Vermont with the "battle" of Richard's Farm in Franklin Center. On May 25, 1870, some 2,000 Fenians, bent on laying waste British rule to the North, began crossing the border into the line of fire of the Royal troops. Unfortunately for the Fenians, their commander, General John O'Neill, apparently mistaking the United States marshal for one of his own officers, fell into the custody of the U.S. Government. The wounding of their other general left the invaders leaderless and by afternoon the Battle of Richard's Farm ended, with two dead and no ground gained or lost. The above photo was taken there the day after the Fenians were routed.

121

No angle of the many-sided prism of nineteenth-century Vermont life glittered quite like the "watering places." There were over 20 of them with tens of thousands of adherents who swore by the curative powers of their mineral springs. The earliest was discovered in 1776 at Clarendon by Asa Smith, a local mystic who dreamed that his "scrofulous humor" would be cured by a spring in the western part of town. He found it, drank of it, applied it in packs of mud to his swollen limbs, and was cured.

In 1781 George Rounds built a bath at the spring as well as a boarding house of logs. These he replaced in 1798 with a larger structure, the forerunner of the above brick building with its surrounding porches, known far and wide before the Civil War. Meanwhile other springs at Highgate, Sheldon, Tunbridge, Woodstock, Middletown, Manchester, and Brattleboro, to name a few, were making their own reputations. In 1868, 14,792 boxes (24 quart bottles to the box) of Missisquoi Spring wa-

ter were shipped all over the United States and Europe to those unable to quaff it on the spot at the huge Missisquoi Springs Hotel with its velvet carpets, crystal chandeliers, orchestras, balls, and dinners. A large part of the clientele were wealthy southerners who did not return after the Civil War. As the spring mania dried up, the hotels burned or were abandoned or transformed until they almost disappeared. After decades of neglect the above building at Clarendon is now being restored.

122

If the paintings of the nineteenth-century Hudson River and White Mountain Schools are any indication, the grand tableaux of nature were much more alluring than they are today, when speeding cars and planes insulate people from the realities of the outdoors. While not exactly dressed for roughing it and not too convincingly posed, the figures above provide a suitable foreground for the far-spreading panorama of the Connecticut Valley at Putney. □ Below: the glories of the Champlain Valley and the Adirondacks are viewed by three ladies from Shellhouse Mountain in North Ferrisburg.

123

124

With the inevitable veranda running across the front almost its entire length of 300 feet; with splendid parlors and a cavernous livery stable, the Mount Mansfield Hotel in Stowe (above) opened in 1864 with music by Hall's Band from Boston. Two wings were added later to provide a total of 200 rooms. For 25 years a favorite retreat from the steaming cities, the immense wooden pile caught fire in October, 1889, and burned to the ground. ☐ High above the village in the mists near the top of the mountain, the Summit House, built in 1858 (below), for generations entertained a nature-oriented clientele, awakened each morning by a bell and a man shouting "Sunrise!" Those lacking the inclination or corpuscles to climb the mountain, like the sedentary gentlemen on the porch, could be transported to the Summit House on a steep and winding carriage road, now a winter downhill ski run.

125

126

On the cool shores of Champlain and the many inland lakes modest inns and cottages by the dozens, like the Lake House at Larrabee's Point, provided the less affluent with halcyon retreats. For decades Champlain steamboats stopped every day at Larrabee's, which has also served since the Revolution as a ferry landing to Ticonderoga directly across the lake. □ The ladies at right at Camp Patterson, St. Albans Bay, demonstrate that wading during the Gilded Age and for a long time thereafter was as fashionable as swimming, and certainly less revealing. Note that the transom-sterned rowboat, typical of the period, is identical to those at Larrabee's Point.

127

128

129

Croquet on Seminary Hill, Montpelier, in the midst of what were then wide open spaces. With her hoop skirt making a free swing problematical, the lady in the center is about to dispatch her opponent's ball. □ Below: Except for the clothing of the fishermen, timeless scenes like this on the Dog River near Northfield could have been photographed any summer day for the last century and a quarter.

130

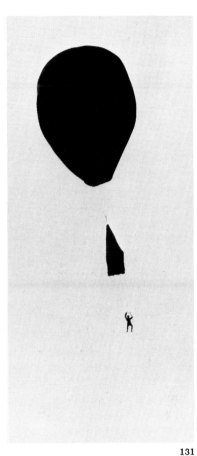

The balloon ascension was obviously the grand attraction at the Londonderry Fair in September, 1908. In the foreground below is a camp of gypsies, whose coming and going often struck terror in the hearts of children who thought they might be kidnapped. This was a familiar spectacle in most Vermont communities until well into the twentieth century. The aeronaut at right was probably "Professor" Clarence C. Bonnette, a native of Island Pond. Starting before and growing up with the age of flight, he was known all over the country and even Europe for his daredevil acts, principally at fairs. During a lifetime of ascending by balloon and descending by parachute (featuring free falls and trapeze acts) he broke almost every bone in his body during less fortunate landings in forests, swamps, on roofs, and even the mast of a boat.

131

132

133

Looking, sounding, and smelling very much as it has for generations, the country fair may be the most durable of Vermont's institutions; it may in fact be entering an era of even greater vigor because of renewed interest in things animal and vegetable. Unless it is the ox-pulling contest—and even a few pair of these remain in the state as mementos of the decades when there were so many, as above at the Bradford Fair—the ingredients have changed very little; even the hooked and braided rugs of the ladies' department remain. Harness racing is still the central attraction, as in Bradford during the early 1900's.

134

The cavalry at Fort Ethan Allen rides no more, but for five decades after its establishment in Colchester in 1894 (through the efforts of Senator and ex-Secretary of War Redfield Proctor) it was a staple of northwestern Vermont life. The artillerymen below on maneuvers in the twenties are testing the latest field radio gear, as reinforcements ride up in the background. □ No pictorial review of what they did in Vermont could overlook the horses they raised—Morgans, of course, a new breed that miraculously sprang from a single small bay with black legs, mane and tail, owned in the early 1800's by Justin Morgan, a Randolph singing master. The horse passed on all his qualities of looks, endurance, and spirit to such of his progeny as Daniel Webster Lambert (right), a pure open-gaited trotter needing neither boots nor weights. The center of the vast Morgan empire today remains the Morgan Horse farm in Weybridge.

135

136

Village Paths and City Streets

"VERMONT'S REAL STORY," wrote Arthur Wallace Peach, "is not in facts and figures but in the intangibles of character, beauty, peace, and traditions that . . . still shape the state and its destiny."

But of course, intangibles sooner or later express themselves in tangibles. The landscape of Vermont, its villages and towns, may not be all that different from those of parts of Massachusetts and New Hampshire, yet travelers are convinced of an ethereal change when they cross the border into Vermont. Part of its uniqueness may be owing to real variations in geology and geography. Narrow valleys, verdant pastures, and surprising lakes in the wrinkles of forested hills. But much of the difference must derive from the living archaeology of farm, village, and town—the tangible aspirations of the past melded into those of the present.

It is said that Vermont architecture eludes precise definition, "yet the Vermonter recognizes the specific characteristics as readily as his wife knows the individual hens in her flock." Understatement is the virtue of their villages, their houses and churches. Strive as he may with every modern resource, today's architect is hard-pressed to create a structure of as enduring beauty as, for example, Bennington's Old First Church, built entirely of local materials with native muscle, human and animal. The village architect, master builder, master carpenter and mason, were often one and the same man. The beauty of his many classics in wood, brick, and stone derives from limited resources which restricted his creativity to comely proportions and a very few embellishments that he really made count. Today's architects are borrowing much from him in the angles of their roofs and in their "shed" designs, adopted from the "continuous architecture" of traditional farm homesteads, which in winter gave the farmer inside access from his house to the barn by way of various attached structures.

The Vermont townscape: the church, the post office, general store, the cluster of houses around the common and green open spaces beyond, have come to stand for the life of a society that grew to a certain size because it could not in nature grow further. The best feature of some of Vermont's cities is that they are yet but overgrown towns. They were all that way into the first third of the twentieth century; early views of main streets display many typical native structures which have fallen victim to fire, flood, ice and snow, time, and Progress. The cities can now claim few characteristics that qualify them as distinctively Vermont. The fortunes of local "squires" and the outside wealth of summer residents found expression in occasional mansions, sometimes whole streets of them. The downtown "business block" is cosmopolitan, industrial streets and suburban sprawls are urban.

Yet the tradition of a people spread in comfortable numbers over a handsome countryside—of a people at peace with their surroundings and vice-versa—prevails. A dying way of life elsewhere has endured in Vermont and may, some think, be seeding a national revitalization. Like its architecture, once deemed plain and unfashionable but now revered as classically appropriate, so has appreciation of the Vermont lifestyle come full circle. Its virtues have been weighed against the offerings of the city syndrome, and the margin in its favor increases daily. It was and is a lifestyle that is the antithesis of all that is pretentious, overgrown, garish, disoriented, impersonal and anonymous.

137

The alluring image of a small Vermont town cradled in a cleft of hills is exemplified by Chelsea, the seat of Orange County and birthplace of two governors. Time has hardly touched its cluster of typical Vermont dwellings dating from Federal and Greek Revival periods. Chelseans had apparently done a lot of living by the time the above photo was taken. The cemetery in the distance seems well-populated.

138

139

Bennington's Old First Church, the work of Vermont architect, Lavius Fillmore, stands beyond Court House in this early photo. Practical yet anything but austere in design, the curves and angles of its chaste and dignified interior represent the cross embracing the world. Much altered through the years, but painstakingly restored, the church remains a classic of early Vermont architecture. According to tradition, Ethan Allen stayed in the fine gambrel-roofed home in foreground. It forlornly served its last days as a tinshop. □ Left: Historic Rockingham Meetinghouse, erected in 1787, personifies the spirit of early hill towns which later gravitated into valleys. After the last town meeting was held here in 1869, the structure suffered decades of neglect and decay. In 1906 admirers resurrected it for posterity.

Windsor's Old Constitution House (1769) was the scene of the Constitutional Convention in July 1777 and birthplace of the Republic of Vermont. Photo at left shows the building after it was moved from the original location to Depot Avenue. There it was used as a harness shop, tinware manufactory and boot shop. Moved again to the present North Main Street site in 1914 it was presented by the Fay family to the Old Constitution House Association, which now maintains it for the public.

140

The independent Republic of Vermont germinated on Bennington hill in the Catamount Tavern (circa 1769) where the Green Mountain Boys gathered to hatch schemes against New York magistrates and other claimants to their lands. For brandishing pistols against their warnings, one partisan of New York was tied in an arm chair and hoisted 25 feet to the inn's signboard (surmounted by a stuffed catamount snarling at New York), there to swing in ridicule for two hours to the jeers of patrons. Ethan Allen came to the tavern to plan his assault on British slumber at Fort Ticonderoga. It also served as headquarters for the Council of Safety during the Burgoyne campaign. When tavern landlord Stephen Fay was told that his eldest son had perished in the Battle of Bennington (turning point against the fortunes of Burgoyne), Fay replied he could not have died for a nobler purpose. A stone monument of a catamount showing its teeth to New York today marks the site of the tavern, which burned in 1871.

141

142

These pleasing facades in the heart of the mid-nineteenth-century Rutland business district before the metamorphosis into a railroad city raises this question: to what degree if any, have Vermont cities improved downtown areas aesthetically in the last 12 decades? Soon after arrival of the railroad in 1849, business moved west into the present center around the railroad headquarters and station (recently transformed into a shopping center). A major calamity to the appearance of this old business district was the burning of the 1792 meeting house. A sports center today occupies the large building at left. Above photo was taken about 1852, at the intersection of West and Main Streets, looking southeast.

143

American House (first known as Bliss House in 1851) was one of several St. Albans hotels catering to a large clientele. The chief reason was its location in the first large town south of the Canadian border, a busy port of entry on one of the main railroad lines between Montreal and Boston. Surviving the St. Albans raid during the Civil War and a disastrous fire which burned 130 stores, dwellings, barns and a lumber yard in 1895, the much-altered structure, no longer a hotel, still stands.

144

Main Street, Brattleboro, from Revere House corner, 1853. The character of buildings suggests little change since the early nineteenth century. The first settler in Brattleboro was really Lt. Timothy Dwight, who arrived with "four carpenters, twelve soldiers with narrow axes, and two teams" in February, 1724, to build the 180-foot-square colonial outpost, Fort Dummer, in the southeastern part of the present town. Other than the Estey Organ works and the Hydropathic Establishment, or water cure, early Brattleboro is remembered as the residence of Royall Tyler, jurist and playwright; Larkin Mead, sculptor; William Rutherford Mead, architect; William Morris Hunt, artist; Richard Morris Hunt, architect; "Jubilee" Jim Fisk, financier; Rudyard Kipling, and the father and grandfather of Rutherford B. Hayes.

145

146

The imposing St. Johnsbury House continues a century-and-a-quarter tradition as inn and hub of town affairs. Built upon the arrival of the railroad in 1850 with a capacity for 200 guests, the hotel was later expanded. Henry Ford, who wrote out his own menus, was a guest many times; William Howard Taft campaigned from the veranda. The hotel has stood witness to every change in Vermont and the nation from the agrarian to the computer age. □ Left: Originally triangular and covered with white pine (which burned in 1774), Woodstock Green did not assume its present contours until 1830 when trees from surrounding hills were planted. Other than the bank replacing Churchill house on the left, the scene from this angle (1865) has changed little. Porches of the Eagle Hotel (1793), first of three inns in the same location, can be seen at far left. Titus Hutchinson House (right), built in 1793, still stands.

Evidence of Vermont frugality has long been furnished by multiple, resourceful uses of old buildings. Tobacconist, restaurant (downstairs), harness shop, newspaper, and apartment (under mansard roof) all occupy the former Baptist church built in Burlington in 1844 in what became the heart of the business district. The church was moved in 1857, cupola and tower came down in 1866, and the first of a long list of tenants moved in. Six brick pilasters flanking the left side of the building remain today as vestiges of its church origin.

147

A mid-Victorian view south from Battery Park in Burlington, shows the ornate Central Vermont Railroad station and steamboat dock lined with horses. The Champlain Transportation Company steamer pier is next south and the lumber wharves beyond. Roofs (in foreground) covered the numerous industries of the Pioneer Shops, many of them woodworking. They were powered by a single huge steam engine. During the latter 1800's Burlington was one of the largest lumber ports in the nation, with millions of feet towed in rafts from Canada to be dressed in local mills and sent all over the world. A series of spectacular fires, the decline of the lumber industry and railroads, and a rise of oil storage depots served by tidewater tankers via canal to the Hudson River have completely changed the waterfront.

148

The granite walls of the Statehouse have presided over a slowly changing Montpelier scene ever since 1836. Designed by Ammi B. Young, its classic walls survived the fire of 1858 and were refitted with the present interior. Railroad passengers entered the capital on a spur leading through a covered bridge. ☐ Opposite view from dome shows the railroad station (right) and the predecessor (1808) of the Victorian Pavilion Hotel (left) which also had porches. A covered highway bridge over the dam is seen in the distance.

151

Mud in Elm Street, Woodstock, has been made presentable by what looks like "sugar snow." Laid out in 1803, the street leads from the business district (note two watchmaker trade signs, right and left) directly into a residential area of fine old houses, probably in greater abundance in Woodstock than any other Vermont town. In the distance, Elm Street crosses the Ottauquechee River to an intersection below the old Billings (now Rockefeller) estate. Other than its architectural distinction, Woodstock still possesses four of 16 remaining church bells cast by Paul Revere and his sons.

Williamsville children slid down Schoolhouse Hill before and after classes (circa 1906–18) until two boys were run over by a truck. Homemade "travers," in various sizes could accommodate numerous riders and would go like the wind. Even after the arrival of the automobile, which ultimately ruined such sport, hill streets all over the state were roped off hours at a time for sliding. This picture was taken by Porter Thayer of Williamsville, one of the finest recorders of early twentieth-century rural Vermont.

152

Putney about 1880—but this scene has attributes of all Vermont towns and other shared qualities better sensed than described. Picture was taken by Adelbert M. Corser whose general store (far right) was heavily stocked with the usual dry goods, clothing, groceries, canned

153

goods, prepared drugs and medicines—with his overflow in a warehouse at the depot. His hobby was photography and he took thousands of pictures of his world. He spent his boyhood in Dummerston and at 20 hired out to Mr. H. E. Wheat, serving two-and-a-half years as his clerk and three years as his partner in this same store. For the rest of his life, beginning in 1889, he was sole proprietor. In 1890 he married Minnie E. Sleeper of East Putney. Adelbert might not meet certain modern standards for an interesting life but he knew the ingredients of his slice of it, those that counted in Putney. As for the people in the picture, he knew them all; they were all what he might call good stock of the kind that maybe made a governor or—who could tell—a dean of the United States Senate.

The blizzard of '88, which started in the evening of March 11 and continued for 30 hours, was followed by a 48-mile-an-hour gale which left drifts 20, 30, even 40 feet deep. In Brandon, the temporary solution was a sidewalk tunnel.

154

155

A pedestrian in Bellows Falls appears dazed at the mountain of snow which stalled trains, leveled telephone poles and blocked highways and streets for several days. □ Manchester shoemaker, O. G. Felt, right, had pile higher than his front door.

156

Winter and summer views of corner of State and Main Streets, Montpelier. Carriages congregating on left side of street suggest a slight traffic problem even then. The Freeman building still presides over State Street, which has otherwise changed dramatically. Signs include two bookstores, three watchmakers (one in tunnel), and mortar and pestle (left, beneath sign on columns) signifying an apothecary shop. Sidewalks appear to be of brick. A variety of facades enhanced the architectural interest.

157

158

Middlebury (above) shortly after a major fire in 1891 which burned the whole block beyond and at right of the bridge in distance. The first sawmill, built at the falls in 1785, was swept away in freshet of 1786. Bridge was rebuilt several times. The business district otherwise retains much of its traditional appearance, presided over by the white Congregational Church at the crest of the hill. Note early carbon lamps over the street, apparently suspended from sky hooks. ☐ In Northfield (left) fire claimed the Universalist Church, Jones Store, and Odd Fellows Hall. But the park, fountain, and monument have survived.

161

Main Street in Barre, in the horse, trolley, and granite cobblestone era. The discovery of nearby granite outcropping, used for making millstones in 1790's and early 1800's, led to a flourishing quarry industry on Millstone Hill. In the early 1830's, 23,000 feet of granite blocks for the new statehouse were hauled to Montpelier over ice on the river. A burgeoning demand for granite monuments brought Scottish and Italians, also English, Spanish, Polish, Finn, Scandinavian, Austrian, and Irish stoneworkers to the 72 quarries operating in 1894—making Barre a cosmopolitan island in a sea of Yankees. □ Below: A single horse and buggy, trolley, lone auto, bicycles, and men share this scene in front of Chase Memorial Fountain in downtown Springfield's tranquil square. A machine tool center, it is one of the state's few largely industrial areas other than Barre. Adnabrown Hotel is in the center. A sign on the telephone pole (left) reads: "Follow the hand . . . Best Ice Cream Soda"; and signboard underneath: "Try a Hoffman House 5¢ cigar."

162

163

Discriminating travelers are having second thoughts about the wall-to-wall plastic of the anonymous cubicles where they must spend the night, and are beginning to regret the demise of the country inn which the motel has almost driven out of existence. Not that a drafty room with washstand, bowl, pitcher, and toilet down the hall is to be compared with hot-and-cold running color TV, but the missing ingredients are the human ones: the casual mingling of travelers before a crackling fireplace, a homemade breakfast, an interchange with the "natives." A hundred years ago many of these early inns were going strong; even fifty years back most of them were. Above: the Middlesex Inn in 1880. Below (center) the Townshend Hotel with morning glories climbing up the veranda. I. E. Chase store is left of the hotel and to the right, Cash Store and Post Office.

164

165

"Man to man," wrote Wallace Nutting, "the urban is no match for the rural mind."

"You can't get ahead of a Vermont farmer," observed Francis Childs, senior member emeritus of the Dartmouth faculty only a few years ago. He referred, of course, to the farmer's wit and sense of proportion. Until recently the urban mind was the rural mind only a few years removed, since the city could not exist without constant transfusions from the country. Until after World War II the exodus of young people was largely one way—to the city. Since then their values have undergone a wholesale reappraisal and many are either coming back, or aren't leaving in the first place. Thousands of others who had no previous claim to Vermont are streaming in, searching for a way of life they do not know but expect to find. The question arises: at what point do these people, by their increasing numbers, destroy the way of life they are searching for? The point appears to be approximately that at which Vermont becomes urban or suburban both physically and in its outlook. This West Townshend scene has almost as many qualities of a nineteenth-century painting as of a photograph.

166

167

Left: A 1906 view of an 1811 stone farmhouse under the brow of Mount Mansfield. Other than apple trees in a clearing or hollyhocks against a remnant of wall, few vestiges remain of many former hill farms. For present owners mindful of tradition the new status symbols have therefore become the number of cellar holes on their land and the length of its stone walls. □ Above: The Peter Billados in front of their house in the "Pekin District" of Calais in 1910. Billado worked on the town roads. Note "eave" troughs leading to rain barrels left of Mrs. Billado. The profusion of flowers in the windows offset the drab surroundings. The house no longer exists. □ Below: The Poor Farm in Manchester. In the pre-welfare days, the last place in the world a person would want to live was there.

168

169

Above: Grafton, 1910. Campaign for women's rights proved somewhat premature. □ Sign on the South Londonderry bridge (below) warns drivers not to leave their teams there. Bridge is partly supported (or vice-versa) by adjoining structures; house at far right is buttressed against house next to bridge. The men on the porch are ogling the ladies, presumably on their way back to their car. It is tempting to speculate that they have asked directions and been told they can't get there from here.

170

171

St. Albans homestead of Governor J. Gregory Smith, under whose aegis the Vermont Central Railroad became the largest in New England and seventh largest in the country. For a time, Smith served also as president of the Northern Pacific, but his thirst for control of an ocean-to-ocean railroad was never quenched. Note the iron buck and potted palms on the front lawn.

172

Drawn into Vermont's magnetic field as a summer retreat were Dr. William Seward Webb and his bride, Lila Vanderbilt, who moved to Burlington early in the 1880's. When her father, William H. Vanderbilt, son of the Commodore, died in 1885 leaving the New York Central Railroad to his children, they set about vying with one another and the scions of other families enjoying similar windfalls in the building of palatial estates. The Webbs bought 22 farms occupying some 5,000 acres in Shelburne and in 1887 built a 100-room mansion on a Lake Champlain bluff in the center of a vast farm, for which the feudal-looking structure above served as headquarters. It contained managerial, bookkeeping, and payroll offices for several hundred hired hands, blacksmith, carpenter, and paint shops, stalls for 22 teams and facilities for all their equipment winter and summer, hay and grain storage for 40 to 50 horses, and a miscellany of other rooms. Two other huge structures for carriages and livestock were built elsewhere on the estate—which remains largely intact four generations later.

173

174

Unlike Elijah Graves Otis, John Deere, Silver Dollar Tabor, Jubilee Jim Fisk, and certain other entrepreneurs who made their fortunes after leaving Vermont, Andrew Addison Buell, who was cast in the same mold, spent his whole life in the north country. He started on the docks at Whitehall, N.Y., with nothing, hoping to get rich in lumber. But more than that, he hoped to build someday the most imposing estate on the hill in Burlington. He succeeded, and in May, 1891, at the age of 49, he moved into his turreted stone mansion, built in the fashionable Richardsonian style. Above is his carriage house, with quarters for the coachmen in the near end; the carriage room, main floor center; and horse stalls in the far end, with a hay mow directly above and hay chute through the far tower. There were cows in the basement. Buell is seen above, with one of his daughters in the dog cart, her pug dog perched on the horse, and (far left) his coachman in livery driving his landau. The qualities that got the Tabors, Fisks, and Buells where they went are manifest in his portrait (left)—qualities occasionally too forcible and boisterous for the drawing room. When he invited his lumber cronies to Redstone, or his harness racing friends from Saratoga (where he spent a good deal of time with his trotters), his mild Victorian wife would take to bed with a headache and not reappear until they were gone. Redstone serves today as a dormitory complex of the University of Vermont.

175

Otter Creek Falls at Vergennes with Pump House (left), grist mill (right) and Shade Roller Plant beyond. Here in the basin, the head of navigation from Lake Champlain, Commodore Thomas Macdonough built the fleet that defeated the British in the Battle of Plattsburg, 1814. Since the boys in the boat are not dressed like Vermonters they are probably visitors from Camp Dudley across the lake at Westport. The Captain, with white collar, is ready to disembark, after a successful crossing of his Delaware.

Occasional epidemics of high water at least serve to remind Vermonters of their debt to their rivers
which carved paths of least resistance through the mountains for
their roads and railroads, and furnished the water power that de-
termined the location of their
towns. Above: Missisquoi high water carrying the dough it has made
in the flouring mill through the
sidewalls of the old covered bridge
at Enosburg. Below: Sluiceway under the railroad covered bridge ac-
commodated the lake that spring
thaws sometimes make of the Connecticut at Bradford.

178

The worst flood in Vermont's history began on November 2, 1927 when two storms, one from the Gulf of Mexico and another from the Great Lakes, joined over the Green Mountains. Since the ground was already saturated and the trees were bare the entire runoff rushed to the rivers. By 4 p.m. the next day water stood in the streets of the capital; by 5:15 all travel had stopped. Within a few hours people in the valley of the Winooski were marooned on roofs, on freight cars, and in trees. Lights and telephones failed, roads disintegrated and bridges departed. By the time it stopped raining on the morning of Nov. 5th, 55 people had drowned. The Central Vermont Railroad had lost 253 miles of track and 54 bridges. A mile wide in places, the Winooski River alone discharged two billion cubic feet of water into Lake Champlain. As the remains of two bridges floated by during the worst of the flood a farmer exclaimed to his friend: "By George, Harry, taxes are goin' to be steep!" Moments after the above picture was taken (from what appears to have been a somewhat treacherous vantage point, but was actually the top of the lower woolen mill) the iron bridge parted from its foundations with a screech and vaulted over the falls. At its height in Montpelier (below) the water reached the top of the barber pole in front of the building on the left. Unlikely as it may seem in this day and age, the state refused federal handouts, floated a bond issue, and attended to its own rehabilitation.

179

History tends, perhaps unfairly, to emphasize such disasters as fires, floods, and earthquakes because they are exclamation points in the mostly unremarkable proceedings of the day. Currier and Ives were masters at depicting them. In view of the difficulty, in the early years, of taking pictures at night, weekly magazines like *Leslie's* and *Harper's* commissioned artists to draw "accurate renderings of the recent terrible conflagration." A perusal of old photographs leaves the impression of an inordinate number of fires in Vermont, but of course there were no more or no less than anywhere else. Still, since most buildings were of wood, since lighting devices were incendiary and fire fighting in the country was at best a feeble exercise in futility, it is remarkable that so many early structures have survived.

180

As late as 1666, when much of London burned, the art of fire-fighting was less than rudimentary. Bucket brigades were organized after that and for two centuries they thrived in story and song. The transition from bucket brigade to paid and volunteer fire departments was gradual from 1865 to as late as 1910. In the cities horse-drawn hook, ladder and hose wagons, hand- and particularly steam-pumpers—with horses racing at top speed, smoke billowing from their stacks, and steam hissing from their safety valves—were perhaps more spectacular than effective, at least by modern standards. Above is Bellows Falls' proudest in 1911, and, right, one of Rutland's hose wagons in the same period.

181

182

A century and a half after the first few adventurers arrived to clear the land, the Connecticut River town of Newbury still had no water system. (The aqueduct recorded as carrying water from the hills in the 1790's had been a source, but hardly a system.) Until relatively recent times most small towns relied on wells and cisterns, which were hardly adequate to fill the buckets of their volunteer fire brigade, if they had one. On June 14, 1913, Peter Chase, a blacksmith in Newbury for twenty years, heard the fire alarm while he was shoeing a neighbors' horses. Looking up he saw that the top of his shop was on fire. It was consumed in minutes, the wind carrying its embers to the shingles of surrounding roofs, they in turn burning and joining in what in no time became a holocaust. To have described the whole town as ablaze would have been only a slight exaggeration: twenty-one buildings were consumed, including the Advent Church, the old Seminary, the large yellow boarding house, seven dwellings, three stores, and four barns. Strangely enough, many said it was an act of God—the fire spared the wooden Methodist Church while razing everything on this side and the large three-story brick Seminary beyond. The above photograph, taken from the site of the blacksmith shop, shows one wall of the Seminary standing beyond the church.

183

After a fire which wiped out most of Bethel's business section in December, 1877, the post office and other displaced tenants moved to the Moody Block on Main Street. Among them were A. J. Davis, who carried "notions, fancy goods, fruits, cigars, and tobacco," and also repaired watches, as indicated by his trade sign, apparently rescued from the fire. Before he took a vacation Dr. R. M. Chase (stand-ing without a hat on front steps), whose office was upstairs, would leave a note on the door which read: "If you have any trouble with your teeth, use putty until I get back." Woodbury and Wheeler, whose shop was in the basement, were coopers. The presence of a barber shop on the second floor is indicated by a pole at the foot of the stairs. The man by the horse, wearing typical "frock" coat of a livery stable proprietor, is probably Albert Stearns, who relocated south of the hotel (Wilson House) at left. Aspiring to present impressive fa-cades, many owners of buildings in business districts during this period put "false fronts" on the gables, more characteristic, however, of western mining towns than of Ver-mont.

184

185

The plight of a hill village that turned out to be located in the wrong place is forlornly portrayed by the Old Church and The Academy, once the pride of Whitingham Centre Village, as they appeared in the 1880's. The church was built about 1800 and the belfry added in 1834, both by public subscription. For years its 930-pound bell rang at noon and 9 p.m. on weekdays, and on Sundays summoned several hundred people to worship. In August of 1857 it cracked while tolling for the funeral of Martha Hall, a local citizen, but was promptly exchanged for a bigger one. The Academy (center) was built in 1842 to stem the outward flow of people and business to nearby Sadawga, but as it gradually became apparent that nothing could save Centre Village both buildings were abandoned and fell prey to the elements. The bell was transferred to the Sadawga Methodist Church in 1860 and the Academy bell stealthily removed to the Sadawga School in 1872. Thus Centre Village (later called Whitingham Town Hill) ceased to exist, while the victorious village of Sadawga, shown below as it appeared before the turn of the century, became Whitingham Centre—a final affront to the fond partisans of a once thriving town.

186

Few spectacles loom larger in memory than that of the circus train steaming in before sunup and the downtown parade before a performance. The 1903 scene (left) shows traffic at a standstill in Montpelier as a wagon with gilded filigree framing a painting rounds the corner of State and Elm Streets. This circus featured the "Texas Giant" weighing 400 pounds (with fingers so big a half-dollar could be slipped through his ring) and a man with a beard 21 feet long. □ The St. Albans parade (below) featured a locomotive astride the trolley tracks pulling a car with what looks to be steam pouring from the safety valve of a calliope, and a second car freighted with dignitaries. The festivities celebrated a century of peace with Canada, 1814-1914.

187

188

189

On September 6, 1901, while attending a reception of the politically influential Vermont Fish and Game League at Isle La Motte, Vice President Theodore Roosevelt received word that President MacKinley had just been shot in Buffalo, N.Y. Eight days later Roosevelt was President. The following year he returned to the state by way of Cornish, N.H., and Windsor in a tally-ho driven by the American author, Winston Churchill. On a special train from Windsor to Burlington, he was greeted by thousands at White River, South Royalton, Randolph, Northfield, Montpelier, and Waterbury. At Burlington, in the company of a great throng, he visited the grave of Ethan Allen, spoke in the Howard Opera House, attended a reception at the Van Ness Hotel, and was royally received on side trips to Thompson's Point and Shelburne. Arriving in Rutland on Labor Day he gave what is described as a "notable oration" before 8,000 people gathered around the bandstand in the park (above).

THE VERMONTER has always been recognized as a distinct breed of Yankee, but his characteristics have proved rather too contrary and elusive to be gathered in any one literary bundle. Various writers have, however, succeeded through the years in identifying his most obvious traits which still pertain, particularly in rural areas and small towns, despite the onslaught of the northeastern megalopolis upon his individuality. But most of the faces in this portfolio belonged to rural and urban Vermonters who lived when the following glimpses of the breed were almost totally true to type.

Faces of Yesterday

The most active and rebellious race on the continent. —GENERAL JOHN BURGOYNE

Just a lot of lovable but pig-headed individuals divided up into townships widely scattered on mountainsides and in valleys who will not let even their chosen officials command them or their chosen leaders lead them. —BURGES JOHNSON

They were a climbing and creative stock who delighted in obstacles, felt certain of their purposes, and proceeded to make over by means both bold and dubious whatever environment they might encounter. —LEWIS D. STILLWELL

Anyone can be a Vermonter—anyone who subscribes to a doctrine of frugality, self-reliance, and humility, who takes up residence in the hills and pays his poll tax—but to be a good Vermonter, native or immigrant, he has to have an eccentricity; somewhere in his background there is a gentle madness, a persistent fanaticism, an honest idiosyncrasy. —W. STORRS LEE

There is only one quality that could be called 'typical' of the Vermonters I know. That is their extraordinarily irritating way of not conforming to any type. Each of them is an original. Born on the same hills, fed on the same beans, educated in the same schools, they have just one common denominator; they are all rare birds. —JAEL KENT

Many a hillside farmer clung tenaciously to his homestead. There were many reasons—affection for familiar surroundings, independence of spirit, love of the hills, some sense of freedom that far hill vistas give, elbowroom, a home from which a man can neither be starved nor frozen as long as a crop will grow and wood burn. —HAROLD FISHER WILSON

Through a century and a half Vermont has remained classless and also fanatically anti-totalitarian. Perhaps because it never had any aristocrats or capitalists to liquidate. —DOROTHY CANFIELD FISHER

The climate and soil may make the Vermonter hard-shelled, but only rarely is he a snapping turtle at heart. His character is more like the chambered nautilus, with recesses of beauty not always easily seen but nevertheless there. —CHARLES EDWARD CRANE

A Vermonter's merriment is not uproarious. It is weathered and dry and flavored with salt, yet no people esteem jest more highly or are more adept at its manufacture. —FREDERIC F. VAN DE WATER

A farmer all of his 90 years, Eldorus Wheeler was persuaded by his wife to return to the East from their Iowa farm where they had spent their early married life. In 1896 he moved all his belongings, including his livestock, in a railroad box car to the "Aiken Stand," an old colonial tavern in Barnard on the "Royalton Turnpike," which is seen behind him. When he was photographed sitting on the cover of his well in the 1890's he was about 80, a gentle man who rarely raised his voice and who was always ready to help his neighbors. Even if nothing were known about his qualities they are apparent in his face.

190

The ancestors of Sarah Blood were among the first settlers in Putney. She was born there in 1808 and died there in 1889, a "maiden lady" known affectionately by everyone in town as Aunt Sarah, because she was always doing her neighbors some kindness or other. Seated in her home-made comb-back Windsor amidst the humblest of surroundings with the sun coming through the window, she fairly exudes contentment in this Vermeer-like portrait.

191

192

Harlow and Henrietta Easterbrook, quite obviously brother and sister, lived on Harlow's farm on Pudding Hill in Sutton. The self denial of a self-sufficient hill farm is evident in their clothes—Henrietta's home-made dress and the patches on Harlow's knees—and in the stern determination overshadowing just a hint of warmth in their faces. They are prototypes of backbeyond people around the turn of the century, as yet untouched by the stirrings of the industrial revolution, living as their parents had, and their grandparents. When Harlow got too old to farm he sold out and he and Henrietta moved into Sutton Village.

"Aunt Sally, the veteran fish woman of Magog Lake, Newport, age 82" is all that has been recorded about this "character" (every town had at least one). She could have been an original anti-establishment figure, doing her own thing and to hell with how she looked or what people thought of her. No doubt she was out there on the bridge from sunup to twilight, putting every other fisherman to shame with her wooden poles, and selling her catch at a local market. □ Below: James Ayer, farmer and twice representative in the legislature from the town of Plymouth Union, shares his carriage with his faithful companion, Bruce—a classic example of the resemblance between a dog and his master.

193

194

Mary Delaney of Calais in her one-hundredth year, photographed at the poor farm in 1915. She came to town in 1847, raised a large family, and buried her husband and children, all of whom died of consumption. Every village graveyard offers testimony that the good old days were often cruel. Scarlet fever or typhoid also could take every child in the family. Mothers all too frequently died in childbirth. Yet hand-in-hand with hardship went an indomitable spirit and the will, like Mary Delaney's, to survive.

195

Known as a landmark in Putney, Warren Willard (1833-1904) was one of ten children of a local blacksmith. At eighteen he took up the trade with his brother, William, who departed for California two years later. Forming a new partnership with S. W. Houghton, which also lasted only two years, Warren continued by himself, and by going steeply into debt, was able to buy a farm. Early in his career he made his own nails and horseshoes. For over half a century he shod an average of five or six horses a day, some 50,000 in all, enabling him to own his farm free and clear and provide a comfortable competence for his old age. Since his two daughters died at the age of 23 his wife willed that his estate serve as an old ladies' home.

196

197

On every Memorial or Decoration Day until well toward the end of the first third of this century, the shrivelling ranks of the Grand Army of the Republic still gathered at the church or town hall for the parade to the cemetery, where flowers were placed at the graves of departed comrades by children. After the local bugler blew taps, they would return to the church for further ceremonies: recollections of Lee's Mill and Gettysburg in quaking voices, and luncheon by the ladies' auxiliary. The above group composed the Newfane G.A.R. in 1916. □ Below: All that is known of this gathering is that they were members of the "Seventy Club" of St. Johnsbury. Were they to sit as a grand jury, it's safe to say no more jam would disappear from the pantry.

198

All of the women at this convention of the Women's Christian Temperance Union in Newfane (1910) look qualified to discharge their duties, and some of them—notably the second lady from the left, front row—quite capable of wielding an axe. □ Below: The Sunshine Club, photographed in 1909 in the Pawlet general store where they met irregularly. Whatever rules they adopted in debating the affairs of the day, or in their deportment, a dress code obviously wasn't among them. The sign (upper left) presumably reads: "Do not spit on this floor."

201

In 1915, Porter Thayer photographed this striking portrait of the Newfane telephone operator or "central," a Miss Phillips. The gathering of isolated farms into the local switchboard furnished a worthy antidote for isolation or boredom, and a notorious opportunity for gossip or eavesdropping, since every line had numerous subscribers. Upon hearing the phone late one night (not her own ring), one Newfane woman was in such a hurry to reach the receiver that she tripped and broke her leg. Later she gamely admitted how the accident happened. Some switchboards were in the operator's kitchen and anyone calling during breakfast could hear the bacon frying. Given an opportunity to choose between electric lights and the telephone, many would have chosen the latter—indeed, most of them had it long before their towns were electrified.

202

Flora Ann Lester displays the earmarks of a shrew, and that is how her neighbors characterized her. She always resented the marriage of her sister Lucy to a man of means, and complimented her on her new house by running her finger along the stair bannister as if she were finding dust. Whereupon Lucy snatched off Flora's freshly starched apron, wiped down the whole bannister, and thanked her for providing the dust cloth. People said it was a blessed relief to Charles, her husband, to die 20 years before she did. A "borderline ne'er-do-well" who never enjoyed much success with anything he tried, he is shown below as manager of Lowell Lake Lodge in Londonderry—a hotel of sorts with cottages and boats to rent. The part of this job Lester liked best was the distance it put between him and Flora.

203

204

Franklin H. Orvis (1824-1900), founder in 1853 of Manchester's Equinox House and also proprietor of hotels in Florida, stands ready to receive the next guest. His family ran the Equinox until 1938, and his brother Charles (1831-1915) founded the famous Orvis fly-rod business. Townspeople testified that it was to Franklin's "foresight, energy, and liberality" that they owed not only Manchester's fame as a summer resort, but also "our marble sidewalks, our beautiful cemetery, our three churches and our soldiers' monument." Among the foremost guests of the Equinox were Mrs. Abraham Lincoln and her son, Robert, who arrived in August, 1863, for a two-week stay. She returned again the next year, and had the promise of the Presi-dent to spend his vacation there in 1865. □ Below: Josiah Maranville of Pawlet enjoys a shave with a straight razor, while Merritt Hulett waits to get his walrus moustache trimmed and Dan Whitcomb, his beard. The well-draped lady in the "North Star" picture attests that calendar art still had quite a way to go.

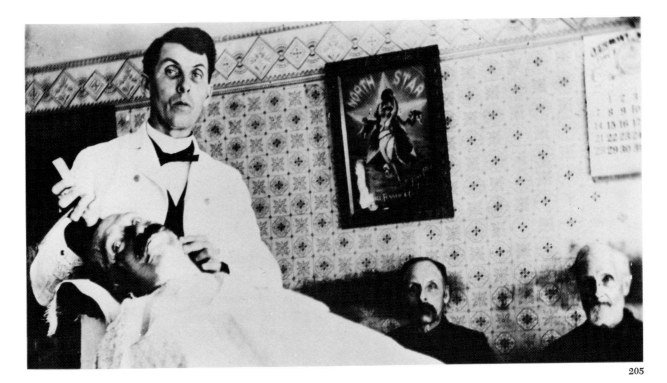

205

206

The Cutler place on the old County Road two miles north of Montpelier toward Calais still stands. Laura, the only Cutler child, was enamored of Sherman Caswell, the hired hand, but she eventually tired of him, went away, and married a man named Gould. Caswell was told to leave the farm, but he came back and lay in wait for the newlyweds. As Gould was entering the door on his way from the woodshed Caswell killed him with a rifle. Caswell went immediately to Montpelier, gave himself up, and received a life sentence in the state prison. It seems hardly credible that Cupid could survive this violent turn of events but he apparently did—Laura married Caswell in jail. He was pardoned about 1902 and presumably spent the rest of his life, a decade and a half, with his bride. Caswell appears with her above, and below she sits alone with her dog—whether after she married him or before the shooting is hard to say.

207

208

The richest businesswoman in the world, Hetty Green, wearing her one good dress and the same hat she wore at the marriage of her daughter, appears above with Dr. O. M. George, her Bellows Falls physician. Behind her is her shuttered house which looks as though she refused to buy any more paint to finish the second story. That would be in character, for when the roof began leaking into a room she would close the door and move into another. Rather than buy a warm coat for her travels around town, badgering lawyers for free advice, or for collecting tolls at the entrance to her husband's toll bridge (right) she would stuff newspapers under her dress. In their patched and oversized clothes her two children looked like wards of the town. (One night Hetty and her son were seen criss-crossing the front yard with a lantern looking for a dime he had lost while hunting night crawlers.) When the above picture was taken Hetty was worth one hundred million dollars, which she had parlayed from the five-million whaling and real estate fortune inherited from her father. Shuttling in the day coach from Bellows Falls to New York, where she was known as the Witch of Wall Street, she would cut her coupons sitting on the floor of the bank vault, and arrange to loan money to the city of New York at a fraction of a percent less than the banks charged. She died in 1916 and was buried in Bellows Falls where, as a member of the Episcopal Church, she was assured free burial in the Green family lot.

209

Nothing is known about the picture at right, which is sufficient unto itself. □ Below: Alexander Turner (at right), a woodcutter who came to Grafton after the Civil War, was well-liked and had plenty of work, but he decided to return to Virginia, where he was married and planned to settle down. But Vermont had cast its spell; he brought his wife and her brother (center) back to Grafton, to be followed by her mother and other relatives. In 1885 Turner built a large house to replace the one in the picture, which he turned into a chicken coop. Of his many children three were still living in Grafton over a century after he first arrived.

210

211

When the literary dust has settled it is likely that recorders and interpreters of the local scene, which exuded the essence of America, will outshine contemporaries whose eyes were fixed on the far horizon. Few if any nineteenth-century regionalists compare with Rowland E. Robinson, who spent most of his life preserving with brush and pen the scenes and people in and around North Ferrisburg. Rokeby, his farmhouse, is filled with family mementos dating to before the beginnings of the Republic. The secret room where slaves were cared for on their way to Canada on the underground railroad remains unchanged. Most of Robinson's evocations of the out-of-doors and of the sensitive nuances of early Yankee dialect were composed after blindness prevented him from sketching or painting. His wife, Anna, is shown reading to him after his sight failed. He died at the age of 67 in the same room where he was born in 1833.

212

213

"Thirty below freezing! . . . The night was as keen as the edge of a newly ground sword . . . there was nothing but snow under the moon." Such was Rudyard Kipling's first encounter with Vermont in February, 1892, on a visit to his wife's parents in Brattleboro. He decided to build a house just over the line in Dummerston, and during his four Vermont years his creative spirit rewarded the congenial surroundings with the *Jungle Books, Captains Courageous,* and many other poems and stories. The two Kipling daughters born here further identified him with his adopted countryside and were it not for the squabble with his brother-in-law he might have stayed the rest of his life. He was only 27 when photographed in downtown Brattleboro, but already famous for his stories of India.

Vermont poet Walter Hard sits on the running board of "The Yellow Peril," Manchester's first truck, purchased during World War I by the merchants for the village, which paid them back later. Hard's Drug Store, antedating his famous Johnny Appleseed Bookstore, appears in the background. Albert Orvis of the C. V. Orvis Company, makers of fishing gear, holds the flag.

214

215

Organized in 1878, furnished with uniforms and a band wagon in 1880, and a bandstand in Farrar Park in 1885, Weston's Cornet Band played for 40,000 people at Admiral Dewey's homecoming in 1899. It appeared for the last time in Weston in the Old Home Day celebration of 1912. □ At right: The destruction of the Spanish fleet in Manila Bay on May 1, 1898, was facetiously called "the war between Montpelier and the Kingdom of Spain." It gave America instant heroes in the persons of Montpelier-born George Dewey (promoted to the highest rank in the services, Admiral of the Navy); and Rear-Admiral Charles E. Clark of Bradford, who brought the battleship *Oregon* from San Francisco around the Horn under forced draft to join the action at Santiago. The only New England state without a seacoast also supplied Admiral Henry T. Mayo (son of a Lake Champlain steamboat captain), Commander-in-Chief of the Atlantic fleet in World War I. Admiral Dewey is shown in civilian garb outside the Woodstock Inn.

216

217

On a fence-mending tour of Vermont during the bitterly fought presidential campaign of 1912 Theodore Roosevelt encountered a thicket of Taft supporters in Windsor, the home of the Maxwell Evarts family, long powerful in government and Republican councils. A political henchman of the family offered Evarts's young daughters $20.00 to parade six steers at the railroad station, with signs proclaiming: "We're Farmers and We're for Taft" and "Six Bull Calves Chained to the Taft Yoke." Clenching his teeth the Bull Moose candidate demanded to know what was going on. "Evarts's steers are loose!" shouted a spectator. Roosevelt shouted back something about "breaking his men loose," but this he was unable to do. Taft carried Vermont (and Utah) and Wilson, courtesy of the Republican split, carried the rest of the country. Above, Roosevelt gesticulates from the train, and below the three Evarts girls in white attend to their steers. (Also present in the demonstration, but not in this picture, were Evarts's niece, Mrs. Archibald Cox, sister of editor Maxwell Perkins, and her young son, Archibald, Jr., all for Taft, and Learned Hand, the great jurist from Hand's Cove, Orwell, who was for Roosevelt.)

218

Meanwhile, President Taft, making the most of his Vermont heritage, visited his father's birthplace in West Townshend, and the grave of his great-grandfather. He spent the night of October 7, 1912, at Hildene, the home of Robert Todd Lincoln, the President's son (left) in Manchester. Lincoln had formed an attachment to the area when he stayed at the Equinox House with his mother years before. Hildene was the unfortunate scene of the burning of many of Abraham Lincoln's papers, which his son deemed of little importance.

219

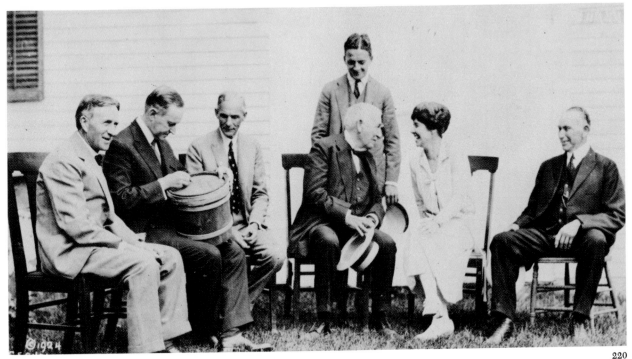

220

Henry Ford receives an autographed sap bucket from President Coolidge at his home in Plymouth. Left to right: Harvey Firestone, the President, Ford, Thomas A. Edison, Mrs. Coolidge, and Colonel John Coolidge, father of the President. Russell Firestone, son of Harvey, stands behind Edison. The trio of Ford, Edison and Firestone often vacationed together and spent considerable time in Vermont. Ford put the sap bucket in Longfellow's celebrated Wayside Inn.

221

Ira Benjamin Williams was born in Londonderry in 1869 and his wife, Lila, in Jamaica in 1883. During their married life they moved 18 times because he was a "sawyer" and had to follow lumbering operations around the southern part of the state. They lived mostly in cabins. While he was out in the woods, she did the washing for the men at the camp. The doll had been Lila's from childhood and when someone suggested she and Ben be photographed with it they obliged. Both Lila's wedding gown and the doll's dress were made by Ben's sister, Dora. The picture, taken a year before their marriage in 1901, was prophetic: they never had any children.

222

This 1886 wedding at Undercliffe, the Fairbanks estate in St. Johnsbury, joined together Mary, the daughter of Colonel and Mrs. Fairbanks (seated in front) and Dr. Joseph Herrick, whose parents are seated directly behind the bride. The bridesmaids included the three Fairbanks daughters, Isabel (left) and Agnes and Helen (right).

Mrs. Mary L. Thwing of Putney (right) was one of the town's most active citizens, leading the Home Demonstration group, the Red Cross, the Community Center, swimming lessons for children, a hygiene course, a yearly tonsil clinic (the doctors operated on 80 children in her kitchen). She was agent for a paint company and ran her husband's grist mill when he was away. She liked to make patchwork quilts for benefits, and in her 85th year made five: three for the church, one for a charity, and one for Bill Apel, who lived alone on a nearby farm. "Trouble is," she complained, "never could do two things 't oncet!"

223

224

The copious sounds of quadra-phonic stereo hardly compare with the magic of owning one of the first machines that produced any sound at all. The Richard Lang-maids of North Danville, proud possessors of an Edison phono-graph, have taken to the field with it. Note the yard arm holding up the horn. □ Right: Turn-of-the-century foursome includes Charles Allen, son of Bradford's photogra-pher, and Joe Vian. The wasp-waisted ladies are unknown. Their tightly laced whalebone corsets and billowing skirts would seem productive of hooks and slices. Golf was then a young sport in this country and a driver, mashie or niblick, and putter were consid-ered sufficient.

225

226

Middlebury College students, ath-
letically-and-otherwise inclined,
gather in a yearbook pose on the
steps of Old Chapel, with the field-
stone dormitory, Starr Hall in the
background. The baseball, tennis,
and particularly the badminton
players with uniforms resembling
abbreviated longjohns, proclaim
their identity, but the avocations
of the others, including the two
ladies, are not clear. This photograph was taken in the early 1880's.

Barefooted students of the one-room Marlboro Branch School pose with their teacher, Charles Brown, in 1909. Some of the children walked three miles to get there and had only a cold potato and biscuits in their lunch pails. □ Warren photo below shows students of several grades and their teacher (in the doorway) who doesn't appear to have stood for much nonsense. Though few farm families were poverty-stricken, few were affluent and a hand-me-down jacket like that worn by the boy at right was nothing to be ashamed of. Delinquency was then no problem; milking the cows at sunup and getting to school before the bell rang left little time for it.

227

228

229

Of the 1,000 one-room schools in Vermont at the turn of the century, only nine remain in use. They have had a long and honorable history, and what the teacher did not have the expertise to teach was more than compensated for by the intangibles of character-building and the teacher's personal knowledge of each student's needs, according to background and potential. More than anything else, the Vermont experience has meant that it is the individual who counts. This is a lesson educators are relearning in demonstrations of such supposedly modern innovations as the open classroom, the efficacy of which thousands of Vermonters, as former students in one-room schools, will certify. According to the Peacham Town Clerk, most of the

230

above students of the Corner School in 1902 "lived honorably," and that, some are continuing to do today. Having later served as a town garage and community cen-

ter, the building is about to become the Peacham fire station. □ The small boys, above, enjoy an historic antidote for the rigors of the three R's.

231

Schools of photography come and go but the ingredients of all fine pictures, inherent in the painting-like portrait at left, remain the same. The blacksmith opposite is Jack Lloyd, who came to Bellows Falls when he was 21 and plied his trade on Canal Street for 45 years. The attraction of children to the powerful man at the glowing forge and the sparks from the ringing anvil are apparent in the faces of his young visitors. □ All that is known about the twin girls, who lived in Londonderry, is that they were the children of Will Beattie. The child tucked near the Christmas tree was Baby Jane Howard of the same town, photographed on December 26, 1907.

232

233

234

Leon Covey lived on a farm in the Medburyville section of Wilmington, and his companion, Edith Sage, lived just across the iron bridge over the Deerfield River. Jerry, the young steer, was given to Leon to care for. After many hours of training he was taught to pull Leon around in a two-wheeled cart and in the above home-made sled. The time is 1908. Leon and Edith have been playing in a fresh snowfall at the Heather Place, and now they are headed home.

APPENDIX

The following have assisted in supplying factual information on the photographs in this *Album*.

Orion M. Barber II, Daniel Beavin, Mrs. John F. Beckett, *Bennington Banner,* Raymond H. Bosworth, *Brattleboro Reformer,* Mrs. Ruth Cabot, L. Barret Clark, Mrs. Leon W. Clark, Keith Cloud, Ed Conant, Mrs. Archibald Cox, Sr., Sterling Emerson, Mrs. Elizabeth Fields, Robert Follett, Robert Franzoni, Mrs. Claribell Gallison, William Gove, Mrs. Margaret E. Greene, Wesley S. Griswold, Harold Haskins, Mrs. Lucia Haskins, Mr. H. W. Hayden, Mrs. Beatrice Holmes, Richard M. Ketchum, Mrs. Katharine B. King, Louis Lamoureux, Eleanor C. Leonard, Beatrice Lord, Mrs. Charles Lovejoy, Mrs. Doris Marinelli, Mrs. Louise W. McArdle, Anna I. McLaughlin, Edgar T. Mead, Jr., Louis F. Merola, Middlebury College, Ken Miner, Richard M. Mitchell, Mrs. Walter A. Nelson, Lois C. Noonan, Thomas Price, Mrs. Grace Pugh, Mary Purinton, Howard C. Rice, Jr., Rokeby (Rowland E. Robinson Memorial Assn.), Herbert Roya, Edward Sharp, Robert Sharp, Raymond Slack, Albert C. Spaulding, Mr. John W. St. Croix, Edmund Steele, Raymond Taylor, Porter C. Thayer, Mrs. Muriel G. Thomas, Miss Erral A. Vaile, *Valley News,* Laura Valyeau, Derick V. Webb, Mrs. Deanna B. Wheeler, Mrs. Lila M. Williams, Mrs. Raymond Williams, Charles Morrow Wilson, Carlo Wolter, Richard L. Wonson, and Marion Worthen.

The following have donated the photographs in this *Album*. Photographers are shown in italic.
Towns listed are all in Vermont unless otherwise noted. Numbers correspond with those near pictures.

ENDLEAVES: U.V.M. Library
FRONTISPIECE: Ken Miner, Woodstock; *Arthur Thomas, West Woodstock*
1. Rogers Photo Service, Middlebury
2. Miss Erral A. Vaile, Brattleboro; *Everett M. Vaile, Londonderry*
3. Mrs. Beatrice Holmes, Canaan
4. Mr. H. W. Hayden, Arlington; *Eleanor Burt Hayden, Arlington*
5. Brooks Memorial Library, Brattleboro
6. Vermont Historical Society, gift of J. R. McFarlane; *W. D. Chandler, St. Albans*
7. *Porter C. Thayer, Williamsville* through The Stephen Greene Press, Brattleboro
8. Vermont Historical Society
9. Middlebury College
10. Arlington Historical Society
11. Vermont Historical Society, gift of J. R. McFarlane; *W. D. Chandler, St. Albans*
12. Jeff Barry, Lewis R. Brown, Inc., Brattleboro
13. Woodstock Historical Society
14. Shelburne Museum
15. Edmund Steele Collection, St. Albans
16. U.V.M. Library
17. Edmund Steele Collection, St. Albans
18. Vermont Historical Society
19., 20. The Stephen Greene Press, Brattleboro
21. Gates Memorial Library, White River Jct.; *G. E. Fellows, White River Jct.*
22. Mr. Gordon Cutler, Rutland
23. Bixby Memorial Library, Vergennes
24. Mr. John W. St. Croix, Hartford
25. Putney Historical Society
26. U.V.M. Library, Dexter Collection
27. Bixby Memorial Library, Vergennes
28. Ralph Nading Hill, Burlington
29., 30. Vermont Historical Society
31. Vermont Historical Society; *W. K. Menns, St. Johnsbury*

32. Bixby Memorial Library, Vergennes
33. U.V.M. Library, Champlain Transportation Co. Papers
34. Edmund Steele Collection, St. Albans
35. Laura Valyeau, Shelburne
36. Mr. Anson Hawkins through Shaftsbury Historical Society
37. Vermont Historical Society
38. U.V.M. Library
39. Saxtons River Historical Society
40. Edmund Steele Collection, St. Albans
41. Stowe Free Library
42. *L. Barret Clark, Burlington*
43. Vermont Historical Society, gift of J. R. McFarlane; *W. D. Chandler, St. Albans*
44. Vermont Life Magazine
45. Grafton Historical Society
46. Putney Historical Society; *A. M. Corser, Putney*
47. Erle M. Dean, Lakeville, Conn.; *Morton Dean, Fairlee*
48. Vermont Historical Society, gift of J. R. McFarlane; *W. D. Chandler, St. Albans*
49. Proctor Free Library
50. Rockingham Free Public Library; *R. C. Bristol*
51. Vermont Historical Society
52. Rogers Photo Service, Middlebury
53. U.V.M. Library; *L. L. McAllister, Burlington*
54. Bennington Museum
55. Mrs. Beatrice Holmes, Canaan
56. *Porter C. Thayer, Williamsville* through The Stephen Greene Press, Brattleboro
57. Grafton Historical Society
58. Mrs. S. H. Vander Veer, Bennington
59. Mr. John W. St. Croix, Hartford
60. Ken Miner, Woodstock; *Arthur Thomas, West Woodstock*
61. Woodstock Historical Society
62. Bixby Memorial Library, Vergennes; *J. F. Cowan, Vergennes*
63. Thomas Price, Burlington
64. Malcolm Reiss, Waitsfield; *H. B. Cady, Waitsfield*

65. *Porter C. Thayer, Williamsville* through The Stephen Greene Press, Brattleboro
66. Mrs. Lucia Haskins, North Calais
67. Roger Conant, Burlington; *George LaPierre, Burlington*
68. Mrs. Beatrice Holmes, Canaan
69. Vermont Historical Society
70. Alden Ballard, Georgia; *W. D. Chandler, St. Albans*
71. Mrs. William L. Thom, III, Wilkes-Barre, Pa.; *Will Albertson, Philadelphia, Pa.*
72. Ed Conant, Randolph Center; *Grace or Nell Conant, Randolph*
73. Harriet Fisher, Lyndonville
74. Vermont Historical Society; *Arthur N. Stratton, Montpelier*
75. Raymond Slack, Vergennes
76. Putney Historical Society
77. Vermont Historical Society gift of Mrs. Laura B. Hayden
78. Vermont Historical Society gift of Millard W. Bosworth; *George Ranney Bosworth, Berlin*
79. Vermont Historical Society gift of J. R. McFarlane; *W. D. Chandler, St. Albans*
80. Frederick Noonan, Addison
81. Given Anonymously to Vermont Historical Society
82. Mrs. Charles Lovejoy, Keene, N.H.
83. *Porter C. Thayer, Williamsville* through The Stephen Greene Press, Brattleboro
84., 85. Edmund Steele Collection, St. Albans
86. Springfield Town Library
87. *Porter C. Thayer, Williamsville* through Vermont Historical Society
88. *Porter C. Thayer, Williamsville* through The Stephen Greene Press, Brattleboro
89. U.V.M. Library
90. William Gove, Addison
91. Fairfax Historical Society
92. Vermont Historical Society gift of Millard W. Bosworth; *George Ranney Bosworth, Berlin*
93. Aldrich Library, Barre

94. U.V.M. Library, Dexter Collection
95. Vermont Historical Society gift of Buffalo Historical Society
96., 97., 98., 99. U.V.M. Library
100. Woodstock Historical Society
101. Vermont Historical Society
102. U.V.M. Library
103. Mrs. Grace Pugh, Burlington
104. Vermont Historical Society gift of Millard W. Bosworth; *George Ranney Bosworth, Berlin*
105. Fairbanks Museum of Natural Science, St. Johnsbury
106. New England Electric Company
107. *Porter C. Thayer, Williamsville* through The Stephen Greene Press, Brattleboro
108. Woodstock Historical Society
109. Vermont Historical Society gift of Millard W. Bosworth; *George Ranney Bosworth, Berlin*
110. Grafton Historical Society
111. Ed Conant, Randolph Center; *Grace or Nell Conant, Randolph*
112. Bruce T. Ellis, Santa Fe, N.M.
113. *Porter C. Thayer, Williamsville* through The Stephen Greene Press, Brattleboro
114. Mr. and Mrs. Alexander Gilchrist, Barnet; *A. S. Hunt, Barnet*
115. Vermont Historical Society
116. Rogers Photo Service, Middlebury
117. *Porter C. Thayer, Williamsville* through Vermont Historical Society
118. Vermont Historical Society; *F. B. Gage, St. Johnsbury*
119. Edmund Steele Collection, St. Albans
120. R. J. Gates; *T. G. Richardson's Photographic Gallery, St. Albans*
121. Richard Shurbert, Amherst, Mass.; *C. W. Nichols, Rutland*
122. Putney Historical Society
123. Bixby Memorial Library, Vergennes
124. Stowe Free Library
125. Stowe Free Library; *H. E. Cutler, Morrisville*
126. Stowe Free Library
127. Vermont Historical Society gift of J. R. McFarlane; *W. D. Chandler, St. Albans*
128. Vermont Historical Society
129. Vermont Historical Society; *C. H. Freeman, Montpelier*
130. Vermont Historical Society gift of J. R. McFarlane; *W. D. Chandler, St. Albans*
131. Jeff Barry, Lewis R. Brown, Inc., Brattleboro
132. Mrs. Raymond Williams, Londonderry
133., 134. Erle M. Dean, Lakeville, Conn.
135. Dr. Balch, U.V.M. Morgan Horse Farm, Weybridge
136. U.V.M. Library; *L. L. McAllister, Burlington*
137. Vermont Historical Society
138. Bennington Museum
139. Rockingham Free Public Library

140. Old Constitution House Assn., Windsor
141. Vermont Historical Society
142. Rutland Free Library
143. Edmund Steele Collection, St. Albans
144. Brooks Memorial Library, Brattleboro
145. St. Johnsbury Athenaeum
146. Vermont Historical Society
147. U.V.M. Library
148. Vermont Historical Society; *L. G. Burnham & Co., Burlington*
149., 150. Vermont Historical Society
151. U.V.M. Library
152. *Porter C. Thayer, Williamsville* through Vermont Historical Society
153. Putney Historical Society; *A. M. Corser, Putney*
154. Mrs. Grant Crotto, Brandon
155. Rockingham Free Public Library
156. Mark Skinner Library, Manchester
157. U.V.M. Library, Dexter Collection
158. Vermont Historical Society; *Hills Photo, Montpelier*
159. Sheldon Museum, Middlebury
160. Vermont Historical Society
161. Barre Historical Society
162. Mrs. John F. Beckett, Cincinnati, Ohio
163. Miss Gertrude K. Heath, Montpelier
164., 165. Vermont Historical Society gift of J. R. McFarlane; *W. D. Chandler, St. Albans*
166. Vermont Historical Society; *W. D. Chandler, St. Albans*
167. Mrs. Claribell Gallison, Plainfield
168. Mark Skinner Library, Manchester
169. Grafton Historical Society
170., 171. Vermont Historical Society gift of J. R. McFarlane; *W. D. Chandler, St. Albans*
172. Shelburne Museum
173., 174. Dr. M. C. Twitchell, Hinesburg
175. Bixby Memorial Library, Vergennes
176. Myrtle Fink, Hasbrouck Heights, N.J.
177. Erle M. Dean, Lakeville, Conn.
178. U.V.M. Library
179. Carleton Wilson, Killington
180. Rockingham Free Public Library
181. Robert Franzoni Collection, Wilson Photo Service, Rutland
182. Mrs. John Olson, Torrington, Conn.
183. Mrs. Forrest Aikens, Bethel; *R. A. Dean*
184., 185., 186. Vermont Historical Society, Charles E. Tuttle Co.; *Frank Crosier, Readsboro & Wilmington*
187. Herbert Roya, Montpelier
188. Edmund Steele Collection, St. Albans

189. Mrs. Gladys Tower, Montpelier
190. Mrs. Charles Lovejoy, Keene, N.H.
191. Putney Historical Society; *A. M. Corser, Putney*
192. Mrs. Deanna B. Wheeler, Lyndonville
193. U.V.M. Library, Dexter Collection
194. Vermont Historical Society gift of Helen Field Swan
195. Vermont Historical Society
196. Putney Historical Society
197. Windham County Historical Society; *Porter C. Thayer, Williamsville*
198. Mrs. Walter A. Nelson, Lyndonville
199. *Porter C. Thayer, Williamsville* through Vermont Historical Society
200. Mrs. Leon W. Clark, Pawlet
201. *Porter C. Thayer, Williamsville* through The Stephen Greene Press, Brattleboro
202., 203. Raymond Taylor, Weston
204. Manchester Historical Society
205. Mrs. Leon Clark, Pawlet
206., 207. Vermont Historical Society; *Bostonia Photo Co., E. E. Randall*
208., 209. Rockingham Free Public Library
210. Rokeby, Ferrisburgh
211. Grafton Historical Society
212. Rokeby, Ferrisburgh
213. Howard C. Rice, Jr., Brattleboro; *F. Cabot Holbrook*
214. Walter R. Hard, Jr., Burlington
215. Raymond Taylor, Weston
216. Copied from "Vermonter Magazine," 1910, courtesy of T. M. Harrigan
217., 218. Old Constitution House Assn., Windsor
219. Mark Skinner Library, Manchester
220. Robert Franzoni Collection, Wilson Photo Service, Rutland
221. Miss Erral A. Vaile, Brattleboro; *Everett M. Vaile, Londonderry*
222. Fairbanks Museum of Natural Science, St. Johnsbury
223. Putney Historical Society
224. Tennie Gaskill Toussaint, North Danville
225. Harold W. Haskins, Bradford; *E. H. Allen, Bradford*
226. Sheldon Museum, Middlebury
227. *Porter C. Thayer, Williamsville* through The Stephen Greene Press, Brattleboro
228. Malcolm Reiss, Waitsfield; *H. B. Cady, Waitsfield*
229. Louis Lamoureux, Peacham
230. Vermont Historical Society
231. Rockingham Free Public Library
232., 233. Miss Erral A. Vaile, Brattleboro; *Everett M. Vaile, Londonderry*
234. Mrs. Margaret E. Greene, Wilmington